FROM LARWOOD TO LILLEE

FROM LARWOOD TO LILLEE

Trevor Bailey & Fred Trueman

QUEEN ANNE PRESS
MACDONALD & CO
LONDON & SYDNEY

© Trevor Bailey and Fred Trueman 1983

First published in 1983 by Queen Anne Press,
a division of Macdonald & Co (Publishers) Ltd,
Maxwell House, 74 Worship Street,
London EC2A 2EN

Cartoons of Trevor Bailey and Fred Trueman by Roy Ulyett

ISBN 0356 09733 1

Typeset by
Cylinder Typesetting Ltd, London

Printed in Great Britain by
Hazell Watson & Viney Ltd, Aylesbury, Bucks

Contents

Introduction

Our object has been to write about the truly great opening bowlers who have adorned the game in the past fifty years, a period which has produced Larwood and Lillee. We have deliberately included only those new-ball bowlers whom we, or one of us, have seen in action, or played with or against. This explains the omission of Maurice Tate, one of the finest fast-medium bowlers of all time; arguably, after Sydney Barnes, the finest.

Maurice used a very short run-up, combined with a classic 'rocker's' action, which led to opposing batsmen being surprised by his pace off the pitch. It was even claimed that 'he gained pace off the pitch', but that was an illusion. The only delivery which could possibly gain pace after pitching would be the top-spinner from a very slow wrist-spinner. Tate's explosive body action and powerful physique meant that he made the ball hurry off the wicket, so that any batsman who played a big innings against him would carry the evidence for some time. This would take the form of a bruised and tender 'v', formed by the thumb and first finger, which had been jarred by the bat handle as a result of the ball constantly hitting the bat.

He was a great bowler under all conditions, as underlined by his performances against several very strong Australian batting sides in 'timeless Tests' on their pitches. In those days, Australian pitches were rock hard: they had so little grass that they literally glistened in the sun, and the shine on the ball would last only a few overs. At his home ground, Hove, on a 'green top' and further encouraged by a sea breeze, Maurice was the ideal destroyer. The fact that he himself was never sure which way the ball would move did not matter, because this also applied to the batsman, while his accuracy of line and length made life possible for his wicket-keeper, whom he had standing up to the stumps.

Sadly, lack of space has forced us to omit many outstanding bowlers, among them the mean seam-machine, Derek Shackleton. Derek could be said to have epitomised all the best features of the English seamer. He started life as a fast-medium in-swinger and eventually became a master seam bowler of just above medium pace. The story went that he was wound up at the commencement

of each summer and would take over one end for Hampshire until
the end of the season, bowling with a precision that could not have
been bettered, as well as always 'doing a little bit' either in the air
or off the wicket. He might allow himself the luxury of a couple of
long-hops and a half-volley in May, before dropping into his true
groove, but a full toss was enough to give both donor and recipient
a heart attack.

The best new-ball bowlers not only come in different shapes and
sizes, but their pace will vary between fast-medium and very fast.
To reach the top as a fast-medium bowler, like Maurice Tate or
Alec Bedser, it is necessary to be quick enough to make a class
player hurry his stroke and to combine extreme accuracy with the
ability to obtain some movement, both in the air and off the
wicket. The fast-medium bowler cannot afford a long-hop or full
toss, although the half-volley, provided it swings late, is a potential wicket-taker, as Ian Botham has demonstrated admirably on
so many occasions.

In contrast, the bowler who is exceptionally quick, a Frank
Tyson or Michael Holding, will find that many of his loose deliveries
go unpunished because the batsman has so little time to make his
shot. Indeed, Frank Tyson picked up a number of wickets in
Australia with a straight full toss which the batsman was unwisely
attempting to smash to the boundary, only to discover that the ball
was through him while he was still on his down-swing. It is
impossible to overestimate the value of excessive pace. It is like the
knockout punch in boxing, a sudden match-winner. It creates
fear, so that some batsmen become more concerned about the
possibility of being hit than about making runs. Even on a featherbed the really fast bowler can be effective, as Holding demonstrated
so beautifully and so devastatingly at The Oval in 1976.

Height, too, is an important factor. Joel Garner and Vintcent
van der Bijl, both exceptionally tall, are not especially fast, but
they are two of the most effective and feared seam bowlers in the
world. West Indian Garner, 6ft 8in tall, has secured a large haul of
Test wickets, while van der Bijl, 6ft 7in tall, certainly would have if
South Africa had not been banned from international cricket. The
key to their success is their height, which makes their angle of
delivery steep and unusual. Their yorker is more difficult to dig
out, while they are also able to make the ball lift unpleasantly from
only just short of a length. Because they do not need to strive for
extra pace, they have excellent control and can keep going for long

spells. They are the type every captain would like to have: the dual-purpose bowler who can be both shock or stock.

Do you remember the first time, as a small boy, you faced an overarm delivery from an adult bowling with a hard ball? After the bowling from kids your own size it was frightening, because the ball seemed to be coming out of the clouds. Garner and van der Bijl have the same effect.

Movement also contributes to the effectiveness of a strike bowler. The left-arm new-ball bowler is able to obtain a different line and make the ball leave the bat simply by bowling over the wicket. Although the same could be said to apply to the right-armer who goes round the wicket, he, unlike the left-armer, cannot (or should not) get an lbw decision with a good-length ball – unless it was a prodigious in-swinger. To capitalise fully on the advantage of making the ball leave the right-hand batsman as a result of his angle of line, the left-arm opening bowler needs to know how to dip one back into the batsman from on, or just outside, his off stump. Having this ability transformed Alan Davidson from a proficient, international-class seamer into one of the best bowlers in the world.

In addition to new-ball bowlers having different styles and coming in different shapes and sizes, their body actions will vary enormously – which is just as well, for it would be very dull if all were alike. Basically, there are five bowling actions, and each naturally is tailored to suit the physique of individual bowlers. However, for anyone to become a complete fast bowler, that action must be efficient, allowing him to increase his repertoire so that, when he has lost some of his initial pace, speed is only one of his many weapons.

The first, and the most commonly encountered, action we have (for convenience) termed the 'rocker'. The quick bowler who uses this particular technique will, at the end of his run-up, jump, turn sideways and land on his right foot. (The left-armer would land on his left foot.) In a truly classic action, the right foot would be parallel to the bowling crease. Before coming down on a braced left leg, he will 'rock back' with his body and bowling arm. He then releases the ball off his left leg and moves into a follow-through which will take him several paces down the pitch but clear of the batting area. Maurice Tate, Wes Hall, Alec Bedser, Ken Farnes and Ian Botham all come into this category, as indeed do the vast majority of pace bowlers, yet in detail all their actions are different.

For want of a better name, we have called the second group the

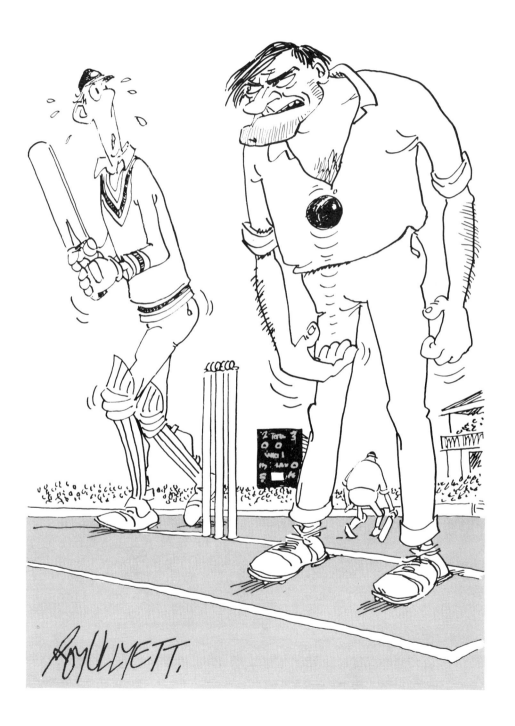

'runners through': those fast bowlers who depend to a greater extent on their run-up for their pace than the 'rockers'. They tend to storm up to the wicket from some distant point on the horizon and virtually 'run through' their action with little or no pause, or rock-back, before banging the ball down. They are usually open-chested, in the cast of right-armers with their left foot pointing up the pitch rather than towards fine-leg, but their right arm will be very high. Bob Willis, Neil Adcock and the legendary Charles Kortright, generally regarded as the fastest bowler never to be capped for England, are to be found in this category.

The third, and also the rarest, is the 'hopper', who is seldom encountered outside junior cricket. The right-arm 'hopper' hops from right foot to right foot in his delivery stride before releasing the ball off his left, a method which does seem to provide a youngster with some extra whip and nip. On the other hand the 'hopper' must be open-chested, while his left arm plays only a minor role in the delivery action. Furthermore, this method puts a considerable extra strain on the knee and back muscles. Its only successful exponents at the highest level have been Mike Procter and Max Walker. Mike's great success makes us wonder what would have happened had he been brought up in England. We suspect that one of the many well-intentioned, if not always wise, coaches would have told him, as a boy, that he would have to change his style because he would never reach the top using that particular bowling action.

Although it is not the most satisfactory description, we have called the fourth category of bowler, the 'slingers'. From a standing position he is able to generate greater pace than any other type, because his bowling arm goes further back and his leading arm goes further round; in fact, his bowling arm can almost touch the ground. Being less dependent on his run-up, the 'slinger' is nor-mally measured and restrained in his approach, but because his bowling arm reaches so far back and his body has such a pro-nounced and prolonged swivel, he is liable to be less accurate than other bowlers, in terms of both length and direction. Jeff Thomson, for example, has always been liable to stray well off target, but Les Jackson did show that it was possible to groove effectively what was basically a slinger's action.

Fifth, there are what we have called the 'toe-draggers'. The right arm version is the bowler who comes down on his right foot, turns it and drags the toe of his boot along the ground before coming down on his left foot and delivering the ball. He does not achieve as much lift as the 'rocker', because his delivery stride is longer. Therefore he depends more on pace, while he employs his body action to assist him to swing the ball. Although there have been exceptions, he will normally have a compact, not too tall, athletic build. The 'toe-draggers' clan includes Ray Lindwall, Frank Tyson and, of course, Fred Trueman.

The distance covered by the drag varies from bowler to bowler, and until the changing of the no-ball Law in 1963 moved the emphasis from the position of the back foot to that of the front foot, the 'toe-dragging' fast bowler enjoyed one considerable advantage over the other pacemen. The umpires, especially outside England, permitted him to release the ball closer to the batsman, because they were rarely looking at the position of his back foot at the moment the ball was released. Our reactions to the altering of the no-ball Law were, hardly surprisingly, entirely opposite ones. Fred did not like it because it forced him to deliver the ball from further back than he had been doing for much of his career. That he was able to adjust without the difficulty so many fast bowlers initially experienced was a tribute to his mastery of his craft. Moreover, Fred's dislike was shared by most of the umpires, whose already difficult task was made more difficult because they had less time to switch from watching the bowler's foot to watching what was happening after the ball had been released.

Trevor believed that the change was more fair and more logical. In every other sport in which an athlete propels an object, or himself, the moment of propelling has to be done either behind or on a line. The athlete is never allowed to straddle the line with his or her feet. What Trevor found especially irritating under the old no-ball Law was coming down with his right foot parallel to the bowling crease and then just touching the line with his right heel. He would, quite correctly, be called, even though his left foot, off which he delivered the ball, had landed on the batting crease, normally in front of the middle and leg stumps. In contrast, Ray Lindwall, Frank Tyson or Fred Trueman would be allowed to drop an inch behind the bowling crease and drag through it before releasing the ball from well in front of the batting crease. It did not seem right to him that better and *much faster* bowlers should be allowed to gain this advantage simply because they dragged.

In England, the umpires tended to bring back the 'toe-draggers' by making them drop behind a line, which they would scratch out with their studs, about a foot behind the bowling crease. However, this was neither logical nor really satisfactory because the distance varied from umpire to umpire; a matter of personal opinion which was not in the Laws of Cricket.

The event which brought about the change in the no-ball Law was the 1958-59 MCC tour of Australia, where the England players encountered a new breed of 'toe-draggers' – the 'throw-draggers', of whom Ian Meckiff was the most charming and effective, and Gordon Rorke the fastest and most frightening. These Australian bowlers inclined to a steady approach to the stumps, whereupon they would turn, 'toe-drag' and open up before releasing the ball with an action not dissimilar to that of a javelin thrower. The great advantage of this form of bowling was that the bent arm enabled the bowler to disguise his slower and his faster ball easily and effectively. Whereas it normally takes an orthodox fast bowler, with a full arm action, years to perfect a really good slower ball, the 'throw-draggers' had no such problem.

Although, over the years, Australia has been more tolerant than England of the occasional bowler with the suspect arm action, whether he was fast or slow, on this tour the MCC party was hardly in a strong position to criticise as there was considerable doubt about the legitimacy of the actions of two of its own bowlers. What decided the Australian authorities to act after the Ashes had been regained was that the up-and-coming bowlers were copying the actions of Meckiff and Rorke. It was obvious that within a short time most pace bowlers would be 'throw-draggers'; and as it was, we reckoned that Queensland was the only state side not to include at least one bowler with a suspect action. But it was really Rorke himself who convinced the administrators that something had to be done about the no-ball Law as it stood. For Gordon broke not only the bowling crease with his right toe but also the *batting crease!* This meant that he released the ball unpleasantly close to the unfortunate batsman, who often did not have time to play a stroke. Trevor reckoned that, as he thrust forward, there was a danger of Gordon stepping on his toe!

When writing about the cricketers who have spanned a fifty-year period, there is a tendency to regard those players with whom you played as, in the main, superior to those who came before and after. Every generation thinks of itself as the chosen race, while tactics change, not always for the better, and equipment improves.

Consequently, the immediate post-war cricketer was inclined to smile a little indulgently whenever a pre-war player began to wax over-enthusiastic about the glories of the thirties. After all, apart from the tactically brilliant, if ethically unsavoury Bodyline theory, field-placing in that era had been somewhat stereotyped. No-one appeared to have thought too seriously about 'shutting up the game' when the batting side was dominating proceedings, and it could be said that this remained so until the fifties.

On two occasions at Leeds in the thirties, Don Bradman, a batting genius, scored over 300 runs against England; in 1930 racing to 309 not out in one day. But though he would score heavily today, unquestionably his runs would take him longer. He would find that the opposition was prepared to give him one and bowl at his partner; most of the fielders, once he had settled, would be stationed in run-saving, rather than wicket-taking, positions; and far fewer overs would be bowled. When the West Indians, with their pace quartet, gallop through seventy overs in a full day's play, the opposing batting side has to average above four runs per over to reach 300 – not bad going against a Test attack – and so even a genius is going to be pushed to make 150, let alone 300.

The tendency to overestimate the calibre of both the players and the play of one's own generation results, to some extent, from nostalgia, but the main reason for doing so is allowing the years to overlap and remembering everyone at his peak. We both played first-class cricket for twenty years, in which time we encountered a very large number of outstanding cricketers. This is underlined by the following opening bowlers: Bedser, Statham, Loader, Jackson, Tyson, Snow, Lindwall, Miller, Johnston, Davidson, McKenzie, Hawke, Hall, Griffith, Gilchrist and Sobers. Among the batsmen we can, without thinking, reel off such England players as Hutton, Washbrook, Bill Edrich, Barrington, Compton, May, Cowdrey, Simpson, Graveney, Hardstaff, M. J. K. Smith, Peter Richardson, Watson, Boycott, John Edrich, Barber, Amiss, Parfitt and Dexter. They make an impressive line-up and, if we were not careful, could lead to us saying that 'There was no shortage of batsmen in our days', listing those nineteen in evidence without taking into account that they were not all playing, or at their peak, at the same time.

There were, as it happens, many occasions when there were not enough Test-class batsmen. This is well illustrated by the fact that Trevor suffered the same fate as Chris Tavaré has suffered in recent years. Trevor was pressed into service as an emergency 'sheet anchor' on no fewer than four overseas tours – at a time when there were fewer tours – yet Trevor was certainly not as accomplished a batsman as the Kent captain.

How we were fortunate was in playing while English cricket underwent its post-war renaissance. England at the time could claim to be, with some justification, the unofficial world champions, something which we have been unable to do for the past twenty-five years. The title has since become the possession of Australia, South Africa and West Indies.

One of the fundamentals of cricket, one which has never ᵣhanged, is that good batsmen will, through the seasons, accumulate runs, while great batsmen will make vast quantities, and good bowlers will take wickets, while great bowlers will reap an even greater harvest. Anyone doubting this fundamental should examine the figures of Bradman, Harvey, George Headley, Weekes, Hammond and Compton, or more recently Boycott, Barry and Vivian Richards, and Greg Chappell. The same applies to bowlers, whether fast, like Statham, fast-medium, like Bedser, or a spinner, like Laker. Figures taken over a decade in Test cricket, or in county cricket, almost invariably provide an accurate assessment of the calibre of a player, but only if these are measured against the number of matches played and the class of the opposition.

To illustrate this point, let us examine the records of Maurice Tate and Alec Bedser. Maurice, indisputably a world-class bowler, enjoyed a long career during which he made three tours to Australia; but he played in only 39 Tests, whereas Alec Bedser, with similar ability and in a career some five years shorter, played in 51. It is generally agreed that Jack Gregory, Ray Lindwall and Dennis Lillee are three of the finest fast bowlers Australia has ever produced, yet Gregory played in 24 Tests, Lindwall 61, and Lillee to date has played in 64 Tests despite the years missed through injury and playing in World Series Cricket.

The same disparity in the number of matches, of innings played, and of runs amassed, applies equally to batsmen. In Herbert Sutcliffe, Sir Len Hutton and Geoff Boycott, Yorkshire have provided three outstanding opening batsmen for England. Sutcliffe was especially successful in his long international career: his average of over 60 was higher than his first-class average, and he was capped on 54 occasions. Hutton, who had established himself as England's number one with a record-breaking 364 against Australia at The Oval in 1938, could not play Test cricket from 1939 to 1946 because of the Second World War, and yet despite this considerable gap when he would have been at his peak, he was capped on 79 occasions. Boycott, who made himself unavailable for England for several seasons and has now, presumably, finished his international career, because of the South African adventure and its subsequent three-year ban, was capped 108 times.

In the pre-1939 period it was impossible to take part in 100 Tests. The greatest Australian, Sir Donald Bradman, played 52, several of which were after the war; the greatest English player, Walter Hammond, 77 plus eight after the war; and the greatest West Indian, George Headley, a mere 22 including some post-war. On the other hand, Colin Cowdrey, in a first-class career which embraced the fifties, sixties and some of the seventies, made 114 appearances for England. But if the number of Tests currently being staged per year continues, this figure will be comfortably overtaken. Indeed, anyone who played for as long as Colin would expect to reach a double-century of Test matches.

It follows that the enormous increase in the number of Tests, and in the number of countries playing Test cricket, must reduce the significance of the number of runs scored or wickets taken. More Tests mean that more Test records, in aggregate terms, will be broken. It is as simple as that. The fact that Boycott has made more Test runs than Sutcliffe, or that Willis has taken more wickets than Larwood, does not mean that they are more accomplished performers.

In addition to the number of Tests played, it is necessary to know the calibre of the opposition against whom a player has scored his runs or taken his wickets. A top-class batsman lucky enough to play in three series against Sri Lanka in the immediate future must surely return very flattering figures which, in terms of real Test cricket, are virtually meaningless. And there can be no doubt that the value of those Tests played during the years of World Series Cricket (1977-79) was lessened by the absence of most of the finest West Indian, Australian and Pakistani players.

It was clearly easier, and more pleasant, to make runs against Australia in 1978-79 than it was in 1946-47 or 1974-75. Conversely, it must have been more difficult and unpleasant batting against West Indies in 1966 or 1980-81 than it was in 1957 or the early 1970s.

Unfortunately, there is a shortage of outstanding English batsmen and bowlers at the present moment, and this was underlined by the party chosen to tour Australia in 1982-83. The attack contained only two bowlers who had previously won Test matches

– Willis, not exactly in his first flush of youth, and the remarkable Botham, who would be special in any era – and two, possibly three, batsmen of true international calibre. One of these was Allan Lamb, who is essentially a South African and who would be playing for his native country were they not banned from Test cricket by the ICC on political grounds.

It is true that the party was weakened by sending to a TCCB purgatory for three years those Englishmen who had taken part in an unofficial tour of South Africa the previous winter. Put alongside the 'life' sentence they award in Sri Lanka and West Indies for murder and playing cricket in South Africa, three years might seem a light punishment, but there is a belief that the players who toured South Africa would have been 'suspended' only for one year if Australia, for example, had been due to visit England in 1983. Instead there was the World Cup, while in the following summer the West Indians were due. The TCCB felt that these two events could be in jeopardy if the rebels were reinstated and the counties predictably were not prepared to risk losing money on that scale.

Since World Series Cricket and the retirement of Ian Chappell, Australian cricket, too, has been experiencing a lean spell, as typified by their team which toured England in 1981, under Kim Hughes. This side must surely have had the weakest batting line-up Australia have ever sent here, while by the Fifth Test they had only two truly international bowlers, Lillee and Alderman. If our assessment seems harsh, Greg Chappell, at his best, was at least two classes better than any of those who made that trip. Further evidence of the low state of Aussie cricket could be seen in the way they were slaughtered by Pakistan in 1982. Furthermore, those of us who prefer to see players who were brought up in England and Australia representing their respective countries in the fight for the Ashes were rather saddened when it was deemed necessary to introduce South Africans. Their presence became even more ironic when, in the Second Test of the 1982-83 series, Allan Lamb, for England, and Kepler Wessels, for Australia, were the two top-scorers in the first innings.

There are various reasons why the English counties have not been producing sufficient cricketers with international potential. First, too many overseas players have been allowed into our county game to the detriment of home-born talent. Unfortunately, it took the Test and County Cricket Board over a decade to realise the obvious and to reduce the numbers allowed per club; but judging from the 1982 Benson and Hedges Cup final between Somerset and Nottinghamshire, when no fewer than six of the competitors came from abroad, the TCCB legislation has still some way to go before it has much effect. A quick glance at the batting and bowling averages for the 1982 season will also show the extent to which the imports dominate our domestic cricket.

Second, the limited-overs competitions, which were and are financially essential, have harmed certain aspects of the game, particularly slow bowling. The promising young spin bowler, taken on by a county, is liable to become disillusioned very quickly. For in addition to his having to develop a difficult and demanding trade, his chances of taking part in the big occasions, such as a Cup semi-final or final, are remote. A mature, seasoned bowler may be prepared to accept these disappointments, but the reaction of many a twenty-year-old is likely to be to improve his batting and become another seamer.

Third, in too many of our state schools, especially those in the big cities, there are no, or virtually no, cricket facilities and no interest. The clubs do not miss many of the really promising youngsters playing cricket, but they do miss the large proportion who never get a chance to play it.

Fourth, there are very few true, quick pitches in all classes of cricket that encourage fast bowling and slow bowling. The outcome is that some fast bowlers who might have become genuinely quick have settled for steady seaming, which is useful in limited-overs cricket and will produce the occasional success on helpful pitches. But it is unlikely to make a serious impression at international level.

Finally, we have a feeling – we could be wrong and we often are – that young fast bowlers coming into first-class cricket have not done sufficient bowling before their arrival and then do not bowl enough after they have been signed on by a county club. As a result, they fail to acquire the control of line and length which is so vital. If one excludes the overseas bowlers, many county attacks at the present time are distinctly insipid and remind one of the immediate post-war period about which Mr Stanley Jackson, President of Yorkshire, wrote. 'I think last season's results showed very clearly a lack of bowlers of real merit throughout the counties. So many runs were made, not through improved skill in batting, but because of the deterioration in bowling.' There was, however, one essential difference between the bowling of the forties and that of the eighties. In the former period, every club had at least one spinner who was capable of winning matches and who would expect to capture more than 100 wickets in a season.

This worrying decline in bowling standards can be seen in the way that a good county seamer like the admirable Robin Jackman is able to force his way into the England team for the first time in his mid-thirties, and also in the way that Bob Willis has remained for so long our number one fast bowler. Both, let it be stressed, learned their trade *before and after* they were signed on by Surrey and at a time when there was not so much emphasis on limited-overs cricket.

The young seamer is simply not being developed to send down twenty-five overs or more in a day and to sustain his accuracy and pace. Several of the young quickies chosen for England in recent years had never experienced coming back after lunch on the second day, or taking the second (let alone the third) new ball against good, hungry batsmen on a placid pitch before entering their first Test match. One such youngster told Don Wilson, the MCC chief coach at Lord's, that he was having trouble with his line – a considerable understatement! Don suggested that he should bowl at the stumps in the net without batsmen, and doing this he still could not hit them. And this was just prior to going out to bowl in a Test match! An international bowler should not only be able to hit undefended stumps repeatedly, but he should also possess the accuracy to be able to nominate and hit an individual stump. Such ability, however, does not happen overnight. It is the result of hard work, both out in the middle and in the nets.

Although under the present lbw rule it is not quite so important to bowl close to the stumps, there are many advantages of doing so. It is easier to obtain an lbw decision, to make the ball leave the bat, and to bowl a more acute cut-back. However, many fast bowlers find that they are unable to get close to the stumps because, after their straight run-up, the sideways turn of their action and rock-back forces them out to the edge of the crease. The solution is not difficult, though again it requires much practice. Instead of using a straight run-up, the bowler should approach the wicket at a slight angle away from the stumps. At first he will think he is going to land on the stumps, but his automatic sideways movement will make sure that this does not occur. Moreover, it will help him get his left foot further across and his body even more sideways on. – T.E.B. and F.S.T.

The Home of Seam

The Home of Seam

Trevor Bailey

It has always been easier to obtain movement off the seam in England than in the other Test-playing countries, which explains the large number of seamers we have produced. The typical English seamer discovered that simply by banging the ball down on the seam, he was frequently able to obtain some deviation. Allied to this movement is economy through accuracy of line and length, the product being ideally suited to limited-overs cricket, in which the primary need is containment. But such a bowler usually lacks the penetration required at international level, where the pitches are less sympathetic to seam alone; though perhaps more so than they were in the past.

Although there were plenty of good, honest county seamers around in the thirties, they were not as many, nor were they generally as effective, as they have been since the war. In the thirties, there were of course many more genuine pace bowlers, among them Harold Larwood, Bill Voce, Bill Bowes, Ken Farnes, Bill Copson, 'Gubby' Allen, 'Nobby' Clark, and Alf Gover. It was a period when most counties had at least one quickie, as well as a couple of spinners, because these types were more effective than the ordinary seamer. The pitches were, in the main, truer, and the outfields were rougher and less thickly carpeted with grass than today. The shine soon went. The successful pre-war seamers, such as Maurice Tate, Morris Nichols, Jim Cornford, George Geary and George Pope, were craftsmen who did much more than run up, bowl and hope that something would happen.

Immediately after the war, as had been the case after the 1914-18 war, there were no truly fast bowlers in England. Those who had been quick in 1939 had lost their edge and their replacements did not arrive until the fifties, when there emerged a glut on whom the Selectors could call. Fred Trueman, Brian Statham, Frank Tyson, Alan Moss, Peter Loader and Les Jackson all fired the England attack, while at the same time there were plenty of high-quality seamers, such as Alec Bedser, Derek Shackleton and Cliff Gladwin. First-class matches, unlike limited-overs games, are usually won by bowlers, and so with this wealth of pace bowling around it was not surprising that England were so successful at international level. They also had a number of top-class spinners, such as Jim Laker, Tony Lock, Johnny Wardle and Bob Appleyard, to keep on the pressure. Such well-balanced, and strong, attacks explain why the County Championship circuit was dominated through the fifties by Surrey, with their strongest challenge coming from Yorkshire.

The deterioration in pitches, which was often quite deliberate – the demand for a wicket on which a result would be obtained in three days without having to resort to declarations – and the marked improvement in outfields as a result of artificial fertilisers began in the fifties and continued into the sixties. However, the main bowlers in the first decade did have the advantage of having learnt their trade on good wickets. In the sixties, the first-class game became slower, attendances dropped, county staffs were reduced, over-rates decreased (without ever approaching the all-time low of the late seventies and early eighties) and there was a noticeable increase in recruits to the seam-up brigade. This last-mentioned feature was, to some extent, due to the realisation by the new generation of bowlers that, in certain conditions in England, a moderate medium-paced seam bowler could be more effective than a fast bowler. In addition he could sometimes make the ball deviate after pitching more than the finger-spinner, who was to be handicapped still further when total covering was introduced. It posed the question. Why strive for great pace, with the physical effort involved – or spend that long, demanding apprenticeship of most orthodox spinners – when an ordinary seamer could obtain similar results in county cricket from less hard work?

This trend became even more pronounced in the seventies with the big increase in limited-overs competitions, commercial sponsorship and television, which together rescued English professional cricket from economic depression. However, it was not until the eighties that the severe bowling drought really became obvious, and even then the number of barren county attacks was camouflaged by the presence of overseas cricketers. The situation was highlighted by the attack which England took to Australia in 1982-83; one of the most insipid and unbalanced bowling line-ups ever to be sent to do battle for the Ashes.

It contained only two bowlers who had turned in Test-winning performances, Willis and Botham, and the seam support for this pair was not encouraging. Robin Jackman, a good, big-hearted county opening bowler of 37, had not been able to claim a place in

England's international team a decade earlier, when he was in his prime. Norman Cowans, a complete novice with considerable pace and potential, and Derek Pringle, a promising all-rounder who, at that stage, was not good enough in either department for Test cricket yet was still expected to fill the difficult role of third seamer, were prospects for the future rather than the present. Meanwhile, the selection of three off-spinners was perhaps even more incomprehensible.

When the era of Trueman and Statham came to an end there was no immediate shortage of quality fast and fast-medium bowlers in county cricket. But in the years that followed, only Snow, Willis and Botham qualified as international star performers, and England were never again able to claim the title of unofficial cricket champions of the world.

One of the best of the 'Trueman-Statham era' was 'Jolting Jack' Flavell, whose fast-medium 'outers and break-backs' played a major part in Worcestershire's winning of the County Championship in 1964 and 1965. Jack was originally a wild, erratic quickie who might occasionally produce an unplayable ball but lacked the control and discipline to worry a good batsman. He became a quality operator comparatively late in life when he reduced his over-long run-up, grooved his action, and banged his left foot down in front of the middle stump. (I noticed this particularly as there was always a danger of my turning my left ankle in the pit he dug.) I would rate Jack Flavell high among the best I faced in county cricket, and in his way he reminds me very much of Geoff Arnold. Although he did not swerve the ball as much as Geoff, he maintained the same nagging length and was a shade quicker; and decidedly more vicious. Providing Jack with support, and contrast, at the other end for Worcestershire, was Ian Coldwell, who bowled big in-swingers in the Cliff Gladwin mould.

One of the fastest bowlers of the late fifties and sixties was 'Dusty' Rhodes of Derbyshire, but there was a question-mark about his 'whippy' action that led to his being 'no-balled' on several occasions. Although he was officially cleared in 1968, it was 'Dusty's' misfortune to reach his peak at the height of the throwing controversy. Had it not been for that, he would surely have played in more than two Tests and gone on tour, for even if he did little with the ball, he was genuinely fast. Another in the fast category was the large and friendly Fred Rumsey, whose transformation from an ordinary left-arm county bowler into a Test prospect, after he had joined Somerset from Worcestershire, was due to his learning to swing the ball in the air. It was the failure of another left-arm quickie, Jeff Jones of Glamorgan, to master this art, plus his tearing the ligaments in his elbow, which prevented him from going as far as had once seemed probable.

The most accomplished of the England post-war left-arm pacemen was John Lever, who has never been known to give less than his best for either county or country and has proved himself to be an outstanding tourist, even when he was not a regular member of the Test team. He could certainly move the ball, and if he had been a shade quicker he would possibly have been a great, as distinct from a good, bowler.

Estimates of the pace of a fast bowler and that of a fast-medium bowler can vary considerably, and some whom I would label as quick, others would nominate as fast-medium. My definition is that on an easy-paced pitch the bouncer from a fast bowler will be quick enough to inconvenience a good batsman, whereas the bouncer from a fast-medium bowler should not worry, or hurry, him unduly – unless he attempts the hook. Of course, the bouncer has been responsible for such a high percentage of wickets in Test cricket over the past two decades that all the fast-medium bowlers have employed it frequently and to good effect. And during this period there have been several good fast-medium seamers for England and in county cricket. One such was David Brown, whose height, strength and determination, allied to an unattractive but high action, enabled him to bowl cheerfully for long spells. Wholehearted endeavour rather than subtlety was his hallmark as a bowler, but when he thumped the ball into the pitch he obtained considerable lift, and there were occasions when his pace was nearer to fast than fast-medium.

Another of the fast-medium brigade of that time was Peter Lever, of whom my abiding memory will always be his long, long approach followed by a confusion of arms and legs in a sideways-on, if somewhat slinging, action. An extremely fit athlete who never tired, even after a very long spell, he greatly helped Ray Illingworth bring back the Ashes in 1970-71. He, too, bowled a useful bouncer, but I never considered him as more than fast-medium with a useful away-swinger when he bowled a full length.

Barry Knight I signed for Essex as a sixteen-year-old. Watching him then, it was immediately obvious that he was an exciting strokemaker, a natural destroyer of slow bowling; and I soon learnt that he was also a promising in-swinger. In his early days in the Essex team, Barry was, on occasions, distinctly lively; fast enough to upset the apprehensive but not genuinely quick. However, he did not become a really good bowler until he shortened his run, reduced his pace, and learnt to make the ball leave the bat, as well as 'dip in' and 'nip back'.

In many respects the most fascinating seamers are what I term the medium-fast and just-below contingent, as distinct from the fast-medium brigade. A pre-war wicket-keeper would automatically have stood up to them, for they are not fast enough to make the bouncer a worthwhile proposition. The practitioner, especially at the slower end of this group, has to be a genuine craftsman, holding an honours degree in cut, swerve and seam. Like a good finger-spinner, he must be able 'to do a little bit' even on a perfect pitch, while on a 'green-top', 'crumbler' or soft wicket he should be a match-winner. Many such bowlers begin their careers as fairly straightforward in-swing bowlers with a slightly open, high-arm action, which assists them to achieve the complete control that makes a half-volley a dirty word and a long-hop a near blasphemy. The two finest exponents of this particular form of bowling, post-war, were Derek Shackleton and Tom Cartwright, though Ian Thomson was not far behind. Their only relationship to that legion of medium-pace 'dobbers' who depend on the prevailing conditions for their effectiveness, and are to be found in county and club cricket at the present time, is similarity of pace.

The strongly built Ken Higgs, with his purposeful, brief bustle up to the stumps, was more in the Alec Bedser style in that he came off quicker than the batsman expected and he hurt when he hit. This was also true of Mike Hendrick, who maintained that traditional Derbyshire length which gave nothing away and made him relatively more successful in limited-overs than Test cricket. Although in many respects he was an admirable third seamer, he never once captured five wickets in a Test innings, despite playing 30 times for England. He was, of course, exactly the type of bowler England needed for the one-day internationals against Australia and New Zealand in 1982-83, but he had made himself ineligible by his participation in the tour of South Africa the previous winter. So, too, had another opening bowler, Chris Old, who was originally a lively fast-medium but had subsequently reduced his very straight run-up, and his pace, to end his international career as a very accurate third seamer.

Larwood and Voce

Some time ago Ted Dexter, who had recently seen an old newsreel of Larwood bowling, asked me if I had seen it. I had not, unfortunately, but I was totally unprepared when Ted said that it showed Larwood to be a thrower. To me this was a heresy; rather like presenting a devout Roman Catholic with proof that the Immaculate Conception had not occurred.

Harold Larwood had been a childhood hero, the ideal fast bowler whose glorious run-up, smooth flowing action and follow-through were perfection. Could I be wrong; had the enthusiasm of youth blurred my vision? Or had the newsreel lied; to be more accurate, had it given the wrong impression? Old movie film is inclined to be rather jerky, and as such is hardly ideal for judging a 'chucker'.

I first saw Harold in action for Nottinghamshire against Essex in Chalkwell Park during the mid-thirties. He was not as fast as he had been, though still quicker than another hero of mine, Morris Nichols, but I was enormously impressed, and it seemed to me that Harold was the ideal model for any aspiring fast bowler. I believe I have always picked bowlers with suspect actions without much difficulty, although a small boy's judgement could, of course, be wrong. But what makes me absolutely certain that Harold was a genuine fast bowler with a beautiful, entirely legitimate action is that he was never queried by any of his contemporaries. And they knew a thrower, even if they were less concerned about it. Furthermore it is inconceivable that in the heated Bodyline series some Australian batsman, or pressman, would not have brought the matter up if there had been the slightest doubt – as in fact happened with the Australian aborigine, Gilbert, who was playing at the same time.

It is not feasible to compare the speed of Larwood with, say, Holding's, Trueman's or Lillee's, but there is no doubt that he was very, very quick. The most impressive description I ever heard came from George Duckworth, who was never one to exaggerate. In a state match after rain – pitches were not covered in those days – George found it necessary to stand over twenty-five yards back to Harold, and the slips were stationed considerably deeper. George

Harold Larwood – looking over his left shoulder and about to come down
on his right foot which is parallel to the bowling crease, so ensuring
a sideways-on action. Note the umpire on the lookout for a no-ball.

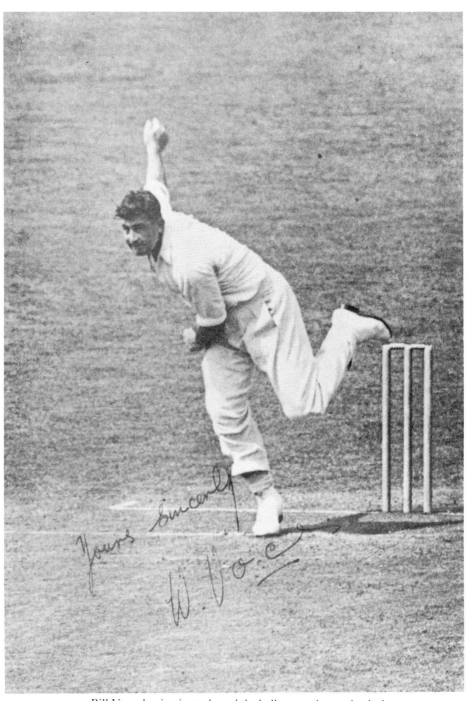

Bill Voce, having just released the ball, moves into a classical
follow-through. His left arm is chasing his right arm across his body
until checked by his right thigh and his foot has started to swivel.

reckoned that it was the quickest bowling he had kept against because of the number of balls he had to take above his head on the rise. It even frightened that perpetually jolly, down-to-earth Lancastrian.

The MCC party that set forth for Australia in 1932 was a powerful, well-balanced side, although since the retirement of Sir Jack Hobbs it lacked a high-quality partner to open the innings with Herbert Sutcliffe. Possibly, too, it did not have the depth of batting that was so essential in timeless Tests on very good pitches. It is probable that England would still have won, although not by nearly such a big margin as four to one, using normal tactics; but the captain, Douglas Jardine, made absolutely sure of victory by employing fast leg-theory, which was to become known as Bodyline.

Harold Larwood and Bill Voce were a fine opening pair of bowlers by any standards. The former, short, was very fast with a natural away-swinger and the ability to bring the odd ball back off the wicket. The latter, a tall, powerfully built left-armer, was not quite so quick, but he was none the less distinctly sharp. For Nottinghamshire they formed the most feared new-ball attack in the land and were the chief reason why the county won the Championship in 1929 and were always near the top during the first half of the thirties. But their partnership will be remembered above all for the way, under Jardine, they exploited the tactical weapon of Bodyline to regain the Ashes and in the process caused an even bigger upset to international cricket than the Packer revolution of the seventies.

Jardine had seen Bradman massacre the English bowling in 1930, when he made 974 runs in the series with an average of 139.14, and everything suggested that he would score just as heavily on his home pitches, which tended to be quicker and even more helpful to batsmen. However, he was also aware that the Don, during his double-century innings at The Oval, had not looked entirely comfortable when, for a time, the ball was lifting and flying. The problem in Australia was how to make conditions uncomfortable for the little Aussie run-machine on good pitches. Jardine's answer was fast leg-theory, which had been tried out by Nottinghamshire in some county games, although not extensively.

Technically it was an ideal plan, which was superbly executed by Larwood and Voce and ruthlessly directed by Jardine. It certainly achieved its main objectives, to win back the Ashes and to reduce the Don's effectiveness, but the cost was high. For while it did not break any of the Laws, which subsequently were changed, it did offend against the spirit of the game.

The tactics were new, simple and strikingly successful, sometimes literally so. Larwood would start with the new ball and bowl his away-swingers to his normal off-side field, but once the shine had gone – it seldom lasted more than eight overs in this era – he would revert to a leg-side attack from a point wider on the crease than usual. This increased the angle of his in-slant. Both he and Voce – the left-armer from round the wicket – bowled into the batsman and short of a length. The ideal delivery would strike the batsman on his chest, if he failed to take evasive action. If he attempted to play the ball down or glance it, he was in danger of being caught by one of the many close short-legs, while if he hooked, there was always the chance of holing out on the boundary.

The points to remember are that the Australian pitches were considerably faster than those in England, and that Larwood and Voce were not only genuinely quick but very accurate. Larwood, because of his lack of height, made the ball skid through waist high, while Voce's height always made him an unpleasant prospect. The unfortunate batsmen were not only worried about the physical dangers, but were also afraid of losing their wicket to the fielders strategically placed for both defensive and attacking strokes. To make life even more difficult, both bowlers could slip in the occasional yorker, with the result that they clean-bowled a number of their victims. Neither, it should be added, made the mistake of bowling outside the off stump, for this would have meant easy runs in largely unpopulated regions.

As a tactical exercise, Bodyline was an unqualified success, even though Stan McCabe showed that it could be mastered by courage and hooking which brought him a memorable 187 not out at Sydney. And the Don, the main target, by brilliant improvisation including moving outside his leg stump to cut through the off side, still managed to average over 50 in the series.

'Gubby' Allen, the third regular fast bowler in the England XI, refused to bowl leg-theory because he did not approve. He was, of course, an amateur and could afford to take that stand. Would he have been sent home if, like Larwood and Voce, he had been a professional?

In addition to the bitterness the Bodyline series caused between the two nations, it ended Larwood's Test career. Harold, who was a hero to most Englishmen and a villain to the Australian public,

The Nottinghamshire duo – Larwood (left) and Voce
– the most feared opening attack in the thirties, relive old times.

understandably believed that he was let down by the authorities. Had he not, after all, simply carried out the instructions of his captain? To make matters worse, he had splintered a bone in his toe towards the end of the tour, and it is generally agreed that he was never quite so fast again. However, he did remain the best quick bowler in England, and it seemed logical for him to be in the First Test against the 1934 Australians on his own ground, Trent Bridge. When he was not selected, it was the final blow. He sold his story to the *Sunday Express* just prior to the Lord's Test and said that he would never play against Australia again. He never did, and a very great bowler was allowed to fade gradually from the scene, a victim of circumstance, the Establishment and hypocrisy.

Although Bill Voce will be best remembered for his partnership with Harold Larwood, it should not be forgotten that he was a great fast bowler in his own right who went on playing for England and Nottinghamshire long after Harold had quit the scene.

The oddest feature of Bill's long and distinguished career was that although he was selected for three Australian tours (which underlines the class of any player, especially a fast bowler), he was never chosen to play against Australia in England. This is difficult to understand, given his record on the 1936-37 MCC tour, when he captured 26 Australian wickets at 21.53 apiece in the Tests, more than any bowler on either side and indeed more than he had taken in the Bodyline series.

From round the wicket, Bill automatically slanted the ball into the right-hand batsmen and had the happy knack of rapping them frequently on thigh or hip. How he would have enjoyed the latest lbw law, for from wide of the crease, round the wicket, he would have been able to force a batsman to play at deliveries that pitched wide of the off stump or run the risk of being guessed out lbw. 'Guessed' has been used deliberately instead of adjudged, because how can an umpire, standing between wicket and wicket, do more than that when a left-armer is able to bowl from the extreme edge of the crease, pitch nearly a foot outside the off stump and hit it. In these circumstances it would seem probable that some left-arm seamers will be returning from over to round the wicket in order to take advantage of the revised law.

When Bill returned to first-class cricket after the war, the beautiful, almost casual, flowing action remained, but time had quenched much of the old fire. Now he was fast-medium rather than fast. Because he was still in the services he made only a few appearances for Nottinghamshire in 1946, and his 26 wickets costing 28 runs each were hardly the figures to warrant selection for Australia that winter. Indeed, it was hard to comprehend why he was chosen ahead of his younger, faster county colleague, Harold Butler. A much better bowler than is often realised, Butler had had a very good season, despite having to operate at Trent Bridge which, for much of the time, was a real featherbed. The Selectors, wrongly of course, picked Bill largely on his pre-war form and forgot that his last tour to Australia had been ten years earlier. It was hardly surprising that he should have an unsuccessful trip, and in the middle of the following summer he retired from the game. Perhaps if he had not made that third tour of Australia he might well have given his county several more years' service as a third seamer. – T.E.B.

I was born down the bottom of South Yorkshire, right on the Nottinghamshire border. In fact I'm only a Yorkshireman by something like 200 yards and my birth certificate reads 'Frederick Seward Trueman, born in the county of Yorkshire and Nottinghamshire'. When I first appeared for Yorkshire, it was said that Nottinghamshire checked my birth qualifications very carefully. Fortunately for me I was born in Yorkshire, because if I'd had to do most of my bowling at Trent Bridge, I would probably be only five feet four by now. The wicket there post-war was usually a paradise for batsmen and a graveyard for bowlers.

Living so close to Notts, in a cricket community, it was inevitable that there was much talk about the Bodyline tour, and that Harold Larwood would be my boyhood hero. Unfortunately, I never had the opportunity to see him bowling, except in some very old films, but I did get to meet him later on. That was in 1958-59 when I went with MCC to Australia and in our party, as scorer and baggage master, was the lovable, former Lancashire and England wicket-keeper, George Duckworth. George, of course, had made two tours with Larwood and we talked a great deal about him. I asked George if it would be possible to meet Harold, who had emigrated out there soon after the war, and he said he'd try to arrange it when we were in Sydney. The outcome was a boyhood dream come true, because I met Harold Larwood.

At first I was taken aback by his size, or to be more accurate lack of same. People had often said that I was small for a fast bowler, in height, not in build, but Larwood was much smaller and certainly nowhere near as broad as myself. So I looked him up and down very carefully and wondered where his terrific pace came from. After talking to Harold, we persuaded him to come to the Sydney Cricket Ground, where he sat in our dressing-room and looked out. Not only was it the first time he had been to a cricket match for many, many years, he told us, but the last time he had been on the Sydney ground was during the 1932-33 tour. He also told me of the time he'd been sent in as night-watchman and was eventually caught out for 98. Some twenty-five years on he was still reflecting rather sadly on that century he should have made.

The Harold Larwood I first met in 1958 was a small man with thinning, greying hair and glasses. He talked eagerly about cricket, for his love of the game was still there and he was excited at being in the Sydney Cricket Ground, which held so many memories for him. I tried hard to find a photographer, as I would dearly have loved a picture of a trio of England pacemen, Larwood, Statham and myself, but alas for once there were none around. Nevertheless it was a wonderful experience to sit and talk with a living legend for the first time, and I rate it as one of the highlights of my career. Since then, of course, I've met 'Lol' on many occasions, and I love the way he chuckles when he sees some of the modern batsmen coming out in helmets, arm guards and chest protectors. Although the Bodyline he used against the Australians in 1932-33 on very fast pitches was potentially far more dangerous than the bouncers of today – because it was a concentrated barrage – none of the unfortunate recipients wore extra protective clothing other than a thigh pad. In retrospect they might have wished they had. On the other hand it could be said that Bradman, Woodfull, McCabe and Fingleton were high-quality players.

Harold asked me if I liked a pint of beer. I said that I did and he said 'Well that's a good thing', because he was a firm believer that you had to put something in to sweat it out. He still has the odd ale and is a contented man who now can afford to smile about the days when, after Douglas Jardine, the instigator of Bodyline, he was the most unpopular man in Australia. The treatment he has received out there has been wonderful; indeed, far better than what he experienced in his own land. This was clearly illustrated to me during the Centenary Test of 1977 when I went to speak at a cricket dinner for an old mate of mine, Barry Knight, who had settled out there. Harold Larwood and his wife were also present, and the applause he received when he walked into the dining-room was deafening. Even more important, it was genuine and spontaneous.

It was also during the Centenary Test that I noticed that some of the scars still lingered. Don Bradman spoke at the celebration dinner in Melbourne and he traced the history of 100 years of Anglo-Australian Test cricket with skill and considerable detail – until he came to the most famous, some might say infamous, of all the tours, that of 1932-33. He then said, and I was there, 'I will pass over the turbulent years'. Afterwards Harold said to me, 'I waited especially for our trip to come up, to see what Don Bradman had to say'. I suspect that there are a few Aussies who will never quite forgive Harold for what he did to them all those many years ago, but Bradman admires him for all that. He told me so at an informal lunch one day.

Harold Larwood's partner, Bill Voce, was a very different kettle of fish. He was a much bigger man, standing over six foot tall, wide shouldered, and a left-arm pace bowler. Although he bowled both over and round the wicket, he did most of it from round, which was then the normal method. He was a fine bowler who had the ability to produce both the out-swinger and the in-swinger.

I have often discussed the bowling of Larwood and Voce with those two great Yorkshire players, Herbert Sutcliffe and Maurice Leyland, who were also on that Jardine tour. They both agreed that though Larwood was the better bowler, Voce was nastier to face, which was also the view of Les Ames, who kept wicket to them. From round the wicket Bill, with his height and bounce, had the knack of slanting the ball into the right-hander and repeatedly tickling him up in his ribs from only just short of a length.

In 1941, when I made one of my rare appearances for Yorkshire Seconds, I had the pleasure of playing a game of cricket with Bill Voce. It was at Wath on Dearne against Notts Second XI, who were coached and captained by him. Bill clean-bowled me, which didn't take much in those days, but all the same I was amazed at his pace. He may have been right at the end of his career, but he was still distinctly sharp.

The moment you saw Bill run up to bowl, from sideways on, you knew you were watching a thoroughbred. He had a beautiful, easy athletic movement towards the stumps, with his right arm and shoulder pointing down the wicket, and a lovely body swing. It was a sight to cherish and I'm glad that I had the privilege of playing against him.

Whenever I see him now we always talk about fast bowling. He must be seventy, but he still stands erect and there's a sparkle in his eye when he sees a fast bowler. A good bouncer really gets his adrenalin flowing. Here was a man who was a killer on the cricket field – and I don't mean a murderer. I mean a fast bowler with a killer streak who went out to win and who loved the game passionately.

I reckon Bill to be one of the nicest men I have encountered, and I shall never forget his coming up to me after that game at Wath and saying to me, 'If Yorkshire don't want you, Freddie, don't worry. Just ring Nottinghamshire and I'll have you tomorrow.' I don't think anybody at that age could have received greater praise, or more encouragement, than that. – F.S.T.

Bill Bowes

The first time I saw Bill Bowes was in 1946, the year when first-class cricket was resumed after the Second World War. The occasion was a benefit match at Maltby, where I was living with my parents. To me, a young lad and an aspiring fast bowler, Bill did not seem to look the part, for he was tall, rather awkward, very thin and he bowled in glasses. Anyway, the big attraction that afternoon was the volatile West Indian, Learie Constantine. When he came in to bat, Bill was bowling, and the first ball went crashing to the boundary. The second was also a boundary, but the third was much slower and the shot had been completed, with the bat somewhere round Learie's left shoulder, when the ball hit the stumps.

This caused talk, excitement and a certain amount of disappointment. I listened while my father and his friends discussed Bill Bowes. They said that he didn't appear to be bowling flat out, and that he was only a shadow of the great bowler they had watched before the war. This was hardly surprising as Bill had spent a long period as a prisoner-of-war, which is hardly the right preparation for international cricket. However, I knew that Bill had an impressive record in county and Test cricket, and I asked my old county coach, Arthur Mitchell, about him. Arthur told me that Bill, in his prime, was always that little bit quicker than people imagined, which was a distinct advantage. He also hit the deck very hard and probably made the ball bounce more than anybody else in England. He did not look as fast as he was because he did not race to the wicket; rather he ambled up like so many medium-pacers and then – this always fascinated me – crossed his legs in his delivery stride before reaching to his full height as he delivered the ball. But his speed was well above medium-fast and just short of really quick.

Many cricketers told me that Bill always knew which way he was going to make the ball go. I found this hard to believe, for there are few of any pace who can say, with certainty, that they will make this ball leave the bat or move the next one into it. It was, therefore, especially interesting to hear what Bill had to say when I told him that I had a delivery which would come back off the seam following a natural out-swinger, but that I did not know how I did it. His reply was, 'Don't bother to find out, Fred. If *you* don't know when you're doing it, the batsman doesn't.'

Bill, nicknamed 'Web', after his initials, and I became very friendly and he took over my coaching from Cyril Turner, and my father. As a result I spent much time with him in the nets at Headingley. He not only helped and encouraged me, but I was amazed at his knowledge of fast bowling. He made me realise that there was more to it than running up quickly and hurling the ball down as fast as possible.

When he finished playing first-class cricket, he wrote for a Yorkshire paper and so was in the press box for all the Yorkshire matches. Because of our close association, he took a special interest in my bowling, and after close of play I would often sit and ask him what I'd been doing wrong. He would tell me, for example, that my left shoulder was dropping just a shade too early and that I ought to bring it round a little. Our many discussions and the advice he gave me brought us even closer.

Bill had been a very intelligent fast bowler who made a personal study of opposing batsmen's strengths and weaknesses. This, combined with his exceptional accuracy and the Yorkshire fielding, meant that runs were invariably hard to come by when he was bowling. He also understood the problems of other fast bowlers, as I learnt on one occasion when I'd been sending down far more than my usual quota of bouncers because I had allowed myself to become upset. Afterwards he came up to me, put his arms round my shoulders, and said in his kindly, fatherly voice, 'Don't worry about the crowds or the newspapers. I've probably bowled more bouncers in a single match than you have in a full season.' It was just the advice I needed and it came from somebody who had been through it all himself.

The best story I have heard about Bill was when Essex, not at the time an especially powerful county, were playing the great Yorkshire of the thirties at Huddersfield. Yorkshire had won the toss and batted, and round about quarter past twelve a Yorkshire Committeeman walked into the ground and saw the scoreboard reading 29 for nine. He turned to one of the crowd and said, 'Who's bowling them out, Bill Bowes?' The reply that came back, 'No, he's batting', was almost enough to cause a heart attack, for Bill was not noted for his batting. Indeed there was seldom any shortage of runs in the Yorkshire sides he played for. However,

Bill Bowes captures the most prized wicket in cricket, Don Bradman
having uncharacteristically dragged his first ball on to his stumps
in the first innings of the Second Test, 1932-33.

there was one occasion, at Scarborough, when Brian Sellars had to send a message to the other batsman to run Bill out because he was needed to bowl out the opposition, not to make runs against them.

Bill Bowes will go down as one of the great fast bowlers, and this is backed up by his figures. But we can never know what heights he might have reached had the Second World War not taken a large slice from his career when he was in his prime. – F.S.T.

Bill Bowes was a tall, rather awkward-looking, bespectacled fast bowler. Although his action was basically good, and he employed the classic crossover technique with his legs in his jump immediately before his delivery stride, his angular build meant that he never looked graceful.

When he first played for Yorkshire at the back end of the twenties he was distinctly fast and very hostile, tending on occasions to overdo the bouncer. And he also achieved some success with Bodyline before it was outlawed. Like Fred Trueman many years later, he was a far more effective bowler when he started to think about bowling, as well as just blasting out opposing batsmen. He became the complete craftsman, possessing control and the ability to swing the ball either way, to cut it back off the seam or to vary his pace. As a result of his height and high action, he was able to make the ball lift from only just short of a length.

Bill was the spearhead of the Yorkshire attack in the great years when they were the finest team in the country. It could be said that he, again like Trueman, was handicapped by not having a partner of similar class at the other end, except when he was chosen for England. On the other hand, he had the benefit of the Yorkshire fielding and the fact that some of the counties were not only weak but also overawed whenever they came up against the 'Tykes'. This helps to explain his massive haul of over 1,600 wickets at a cost of under 17 apiece.

There are various reasons why a bowler of his ability and results, in terms of wickets taken, should have made only fifteen appearances for England, other than the obvious one that there were fewer Tests than there are today. In the thirties, England had a number of fine fast bowlers, and so the competition for places was fierce, especially as only two fast bowlers were normally included in a Test side. However, at home, from 1934 to the commencement of the war, Bill was more or less a regular choice to open the bowling. What I find strange, though, is that he made only one overseas tour, with Jardine in 1932-33. It is true that he played in only one Test and captured only one wicket, but he was kept out by Larwood and Voce, who bowled Bodyline more effectively, and by G. O. Allen, who was an all-rounder. Furthermore he had not then reached his peak, so why didn't he go again?

Although I saw Bill Bowes bowling against Essex before the war, I did not face him until 1947 when he came to Fenner's with Yorkshire. It was also the first time I bowled at Hutton, who in the county's second innings produced a masterly, undefeated century. The surprising feature was that, having dismissed the county for 246 in the first innings, the University should have made over 400 in reply. As this included my first hundred at that level of the game, I was able to study Bill with great care and interest from the best possible position.

His pace was not much above medium, which as he had been a P.O.W. was to be expected, and as a result his 'nip-backer' took the inside edge, rather than hitting the pad, and anything short on that benign Fenner's wicket stood up and looked at you quizzically instead of hustling through. Nevertheless, it was easy to appreciate his control and the thought that went into each delivery. Like all the best Yorkshire bowlers, he was mean to batsmen, giving nought away, and his 35 overs cost only 65 runs. Every one had to be worked for, and I was thankful that Bill was well past his prime. Still, it was a wonderful experience to bat against one of the great, thinking fast bowlers; and even if the pace had gone, that nasty nagging length remained. – T.E.B.

Ken Farnes

My first visit to Lord's coincided with my first sight of Ken Farnes in action, and I am still not certain which made the most impression. The occasion was the University Match of 1933, which in those days was one of the most important fixtures of the season and which nobody, let alone the captain, would have considered deliberately missing in order to play for England. Denys Wilcox captained Cambridge and the cricketers from my Prep school, which had been founded by his father and of which he was himself to become headmaster, were taken along.

I was a very small boy and therefore it was not surprising that it was the height of Farnes which fascinated me most. He was six feet five, slim but powerfully built, and to me he seemed a giant. It was only later, when he was playing for Essex, that I began to appreciate his ability as a bowler. His run-up was short, even by pre-war standards, and straight. His approach was brisk, a high-stepping canter rather than a gallop, and his action was very high, which enabled him to achieve unpleasant lift from most pitches. He used a very loose, flipping right wrist to produce even more nip. He did not swing the ball to any extent, nor was he able to move it off the seam with the same consistency and intent as his Essex colleague, Nichols, but his pace was very fast and he clearly had no love of opposing batsmen. His main weapons were, like those of Bob Willis forty years later, pace and bounce.

I was fortunate to see Ken Farnes on many occasions for Essex, usually during the school holidays, when he formed with Morris Nichols one of the most effective opening attacks in the country. Indeed, Essex in the thirties could boast a remarkable collection of high-class seam bowlers, for in addition to Nichols and Farnes there were Ray Smith, 'Hopper' Read and Colonel J. W. T. A. Stephenson. It is an impressive list, but as Farnes, Read and Stephenson were amateurs, it was never feasible to include them in the same team.

Denys Wilcox told me that although Nichols, Farnes and Read were a most formidable pace trio – Nichols did the most off the pitch, Farnes achieved the greatest lift, and Read was the quickest through the air – they only once played in the same Essex side.

Coming down from his jump, Ken Farnes is already looking over
his left shoulder and his back is beginning to arch.

That, apparently, was against Gloucestershire, and while I have not checked this thoroughly, certainly the appearance of all three was rare. Shortly after tea in this match at Gloucester, Denys opened with Nichols and Farnes, and then as first change brought on Read, who proceeded to mark out a run-up which was far longer than those used by the other two. When 'Hopper' set off on his run his knees appeared almost to hit his chin, which was too much for the crowd, who roared with laughter. The indignant bowler's response was to bowl with such speed and fury that the batsmen, among them Wally Hammond, reckoned they had never seen anything faster in England.

I have often wondered how the pace of those few overs from Read compared with a much more famous occasion at Lord's in the 1938 Gentlemen v Players match. On that occasion Farnes, unhappy about being omitted from the England side, roared in for a first over of frightening speed, in which Bill Edrich and the night-watchman departed, and demolished the Players' first innings with figures of eight for 43. Farnes, in fact, enjoyed considerable success in Gents v Players matches, a sure indication of his class, as he was bowling against some of the finest batsmen in the world.

Although Ken Farnes performed many remarkable bowling feats for his county, including capturing 11 wickets in the totally unexpected and rare Essex victory over Yorkshire in 1934, he will be best remembered for his feats in Test cricket. In a decade of first-class cricket at a time when every good county, let alone an international, bowler expected to capture over 100 wickets in a full first-class season, he took only a combined total of 720. His first Test was in 1934 against Australia at Trent Bridge, where he had the distinction of capturing five wickets in each innings and yet finished on the losing side by the very considerable margin of over 230 runs.

He made fifteen appearances for England, which was probably about par for the course for a really good fast bowler, especially one who was not available for selection in the first part of the summer because of his school-mastering commitments. In addition he went on three overseas tours, and it was on one of these, to Australia in 1936-37, that he performed what was unquestionably his greatest bowling feat. On a magnificent Melbourne pitch he took six for 96 as Australia amassed a first-innings total of 604 runs and went on to defeat England by an innings and 200 runs.

Farnes was at his peak between 1934 and 1939. If he had not been killed during the war in a flying accident, he might possibly have been able to provide England with some of the pace that was lacking post-war until the new generation of quickies arrived. However, it should be remembered that he would have been in his mid-thirties by then.

Ken Farnes was third among my childhood fast-bowling heroes. First came Larwood – after all he had played a decisive part in winning two series against Australia. My second choice was the indestructable Morris Nichols, with his long, splay-footed, shanking run and rather ugly action; and yet he was an expert ballroom dancer. Although not as fast as Farnes, he was more deadly on a green wicket and was also an accomplished and dependable batsman. Then came Farnes who, in addition to his bowling, epitomised the tall, dark, handsome hero of the romantic novel. He had the looks which men remember and women never forget. – T.E.B.

Although I never had the fortune to see the England and Essex fast bowler, Ken Farnes, in action, I can just recall meeting him. My father used to play for the village cricket club at Stainton, and in those days there was a match against Worksop College, where Ken Farnes was one of the masters. I was, at the time, a lad of about seven or eight and, not surprisingly, I remember him as a real giant. But that was how, on a summer's day in 1938, I walked down the road to Worksop with my father on one side and Ken Farnes on the other, holding their hands while they talked about the gathering war-clouds. Their talk meant nothing to me. What was really important was that I was actually touching an England fast bowler, a god.

Farnes died three years later in an air crash while training with the RAF, and his death was a great loss for English cricket. Had this tragedy not occurred, I could well have had the opportunity of playing for Yorkshire against him, for he would certainly have continued playing after the war. It would have been a great thrill for me; but as it is, all I have is the memory of a small boy meeting a cricketing giant. – F.S.T.

Alec Bedser

People often ask who your first wicket in Test cricket was, which is easy to remember, but you rarely hear them ask 'Who was your first bowling partner?' Well, I can remember that even better, because it was Alec Bedser, better known as 'Big Al', or the 'Big Fella'. In my opinion he was the greatest fast-medium bowler of my era and he will certainly go down as one of the game's immortals. His record of 236 wickets becomes far more remarkable when you take into account the quality of the opposition he bowled against, and that for much of his career there was no class support at the other end.

Alec was one of the few bowlers I have known who had a sideways-on action but bowled the in-swinger, making the ball dip in very late, go a long way and bounce. With Len Hutton he worked out a method of dismissing Don Bradman. He would place Len just behind square on the leg side, and he trapped the Don there on several occasions. Because he knew how to bowl to his field, you could afford to stand very close without being in danger, for his aim was to make the batsman play every ball. Later in his career he became even more effective, because in addition to pushing the ball away from the bat, as a contrast to his in-swing, he mastered probably the best leg-cutter of all time.

You will hear Australians describe a certain delivery as a leg-cutter, which I would call a seamer. The leg-cutter that Alec bowled was very different. His hand was pulled across the seam, and with the aid of the fingers it was really a fast leg-break. Alec was helped by having enormous hands and fingers which were so large that when he placed the ball inside them it could not be seen. Bowling his leg-cutters on a rain-affected wicket, or a dusty one, he could be virtually unplayable. The ball would dip into the batsman at a very lively fast-medium, and immediately after it had pitched it would cut back sharply towards the off. No batsman in the world really has an answer to the delivery which starts outside off stump, pitches leg stump, and hits the top of the off. The most impressive genuine leg-cutters I have seen, apart from those from Alec, were bowled by the England and Derbyshire bowler, George Pope.

Essentially a nice person, easy to get on with and to talk to, Alec

47

Absolute perfection as Alec Bedser moves into his delivery stride.
It is impossible to imagine a better action for a fast medium
bowler with a big-frame.

was another who drank a pint of beer and thought you needed
something inside you to sweat out when you bowled. He was, in
fact, never really happy unless he was bowling, and believed that
when you started bowling at the beginning of the season you
carried on until the end. In this time he expected to send down
well over a thousand overs. His run-up may have looked a little
laboured, but I suspect this was simply an illusion brought about
by his massive frame. In his body action, the 'Big Fella' pulled
himself up to his full height before swinging those immense shoulders
round as he delivered the ball.

When I played my first Test for England, against India in 1952,
I shared the new ball with Alec. It was not until the second innings
that we got things right. In the first, as the young aspiring fast
bowler, I had to bowl up the hill at Headingley, but we switched
round in the second and from then we became great mates. What I
found particularly helpful about Alec was that he was always
willing to give advice on how to bowl at certain batsmen and the
best field to set, or to give the right comfort and advice when things
went wrong.

For his Benefit match in 1953, Alec chose the Yorkshire game,
for in those days we did draw the crowds. I was in the Air Force
then, and Alec wrote to my commanding officer to ask if I could
play. As England's new fast bowler who had routed the Indians, I
had become news and therefore was an additional attraction. My
C.O., Jim Warfield, sent for me and said, 'Alec Bedser wants you to
play for Yorkshire against Surrey at The Oval. I don't know why,
but he does, and so I've given you time off. I have informed both
your Secretary, John Nash, and your captain, Norman Yardley, so
you'll be playing at The Oval on Saturday.'

This was marvellous news: a weekend away from the RAF,
doing what I enjoyed most and also getting paid for it. Surrey were
in the second year of their seven successive County Championships
and The Oval was packed when I arrived. The pitch was a white,
bare-looking strip, but Alec had been assured by the groundsman
that it was possibly the best wicket he had ever made. This was
what Alec wanted. Being a businessman, he knew how essential it
was for him that the game went the full three days.

Having won the toss, Yorkshire batted and opened with Len
Hutton and Frank Lowson. After a few overs Stuart Surridge
decided that Alec and Peter Loader should swop ends and so Jim
Laker was put on for one over from the Vauxhall End. Immediately

he turned the ball square, although he said that he was not even trying to spin it. I shall never forget the consternation on Alec's face. He could not believe what he had seen, and the look he threw towards the groundsman's hut was enough to have demolished it along with all the occupants. Instead of an easy-paced pitch which would produce thousands of runs, the match was played on a 'turner' and was all over by the third morning. Alec was delighted that Surrey beat Yorkshire, but he was not so happy that it happened so quickly. That cost him money.

I was lucky to have had a bowler like Alec Bedser at the other end on my Test début, and I don't believe I'll see the likes of him again in my lifetime. – F.S.T.

There can be no doubt that Alec Bedser was the finest post-war fast-medium bowler, and he ranks alongside the immortals of other eras, possibly just ahead of Maurice Tate and just behind Sydney Barnes. He stood, both literally and figuratively, above all the others of his breed.

Alec surged up to the wicket, not especially quickly, but so strongly that it would have taken an anti-tank gun to stop him reaching his classical action. This would have served as a model for any young bowler. Everything was correct; arms, shoulders, body and feet, with his right foot coming down behind and parallel to the bowling crease and his left foot pointing to fine-leg before he swivelled as he released the ball. Although these characteristics suggested an away-swinger, curiously Alec's stock delivery was the in-swinger, which dipped in very late and brought him numerous victims, either 'bowled through the gate' as they attempted to drive him through the covers or caught at backward short-leg, usually off the inside edge.

Although Alec was not fast, about Ian Botham's pace, he did come off the pitch quicker than one expected because of his fine body action and perfect timing. Consequently a batsman, after a long innings against him, would usually have a bruised right hand as a result of the constant jarring from the bat handle after the ball had hit the blade. He wanted the wicket-keeper standing up to the stumps, not back as even medium-pacers so often have today, and this meant that he never had to strain for extra pace. It also provided him with another aiming mark and hemmed in the batsman. He was fortunate in having the invaluable assistance of two high-quality 'keepers in Godfrey Evans for England and Arthur

McIntyre for Surrey. One of the great sights of the game was to see either of them taking Alec on a pitch that was giving some help, with the ball cutting off the seam and frequently bouncing shoulder high.

I especially treasure two catches which Godfrey took off Alec. The first was in a Test during the 1950-51 Australian tour, when Neil Harvey produced a genuine leg-glance, not a tickle, and was caught airborne and at full length down the leg side. The other was in the comparatively relaxed, and unimportant, atmosphere of the Scarborough Festival. Billy Sutcliffe played his leg-glide off the middle and if Godfrey had been standing back it would have been far too wide to catch. But he was standing up, and dived to take the ball left-handed and parallel to the ground. Those were two of the rare occasions when one felt genuinely sorry for an opposing batsman.

Alec maintained a full length, especially with the new ball, and attacked the stumps, so forcing the batsman to play almost every delivery. Pinning him down accurately, he worried him with movement both in the air and off the seam and occasionally deceived him with a cleverly disguised slower ball that was seldom picked until it had been released.

I once put my hand in Alec's vast palm in order to measure the size of our fingers. Mine just reached the first joints on his. This was one of the reasons why he was able to cut and spin his famous leg-cutter so much that in certain conditions he was close to unplayable. On one occasion at The Oval he bowled five leg-cutters in succession to Doug Insole, while I watched appreciatively from the other end and was extremely thankful to be there. Four dipped in late, pitched around middle and leg, and went over the top of the off as Doug played and missed. The fifth Doug managed to edge at catchable height through the slips to the boundary. This brought forth a typical Alec lament: 'I always thought you were a lucky player and now I've proved it.'

What made Alec's leg-cutter so much more effective than that of any other bowler was the pace and the accuracy with which he bowled it, combined with the fact that it would occasionally bite and turn on a plumb wicket. Even when it failed to do this there was that disconcerting feeling that it might.

After the war there was a shortage of outstanding bowlers. The majority of those who had been playing county cricket in the thirties had lost some of their bite, or were on the decline, while the newcomers had not matured sufficiently. Alec, who had been on the Surrey staff before the outbreak of hostilities, without holding a place in a strong county XI, was the first to emerge. Initially he was a big-hearted, big-shouldered stock bowler whose late in-swerve made him dangerous with the new ball and who could be relied on to plug away for long spells without giving anything away. In those days he suffered from the lack of class at the other end when bowling for both Surrey and England, and this could hardly be better illustrated by the fact that, on his first Australian tour in 1946-47, the England attack contained only two bowlers of international calibre – Alec himself and the enigmatic Doug Wright. The outcome of this was that Alec was called upon by Wally Hammond to undertake numerous marathon spells on easy-paced pitches, against high-class batsmen, in heat which would have destroyed a smaller or less-determined man.

Although this tour firmly established Alec as an England regular and a dependable stock bowler, it took several years for him to develop from an honest tradesman into a master craftsman. When he added surely the best of all leg-cutters to his considerable repertoire, this gave him another dimension. He did not really reach his peak until the early fifties.

As with Fred, Alec was my first new-ball partner for England, and I also opened the bowling with him throughout my first trip to Australia in 1950-51 when, with not a very good team, we came closer to beating a powerful Australia than is sometimes realised. This gave me the opportunity to watch Alec at close quarters, and I also benefited greatly from his accuracy because batsmen were usually pleased to come to my end and were prepared to play the odd risky stroke – something they would never have tried off him.

I also came to appreciate Alec's determination, control and dry sense of humour. This was typified in a comment he made as he passed me at mid-off on his way back to his mark before sending down his thirtieth eight-ball over. 'Just received a cable from Brian Castor [the Surrey Secretary at that time], Trev,' he said, 'telling me to keep myself fresh for Surrey'.

It was still the time of rationing and we sent food parcels home throughout that tour. Just before the end of our visit, the players decided that it would be a good idea if a large parcel of 'goodies' for each member of the party could be put on board the ship on which some of the team were returning to England. Alec, who seemed to be on good terms with every businessman in Australia, was unanimously put in charge of the operation and I was sent along as his assistant. Thanks to him, the expedition proved to be an unqualified success, which is why I was not surprised that the Bedser twins, when they retired from the game, were so successful in the commercial world. Quite apart from Alec's charm, everybody has always liked and respected him, while unlike myself, who can never remember a name, Alec never seems to forget one.

In Australia, where their seamers tend to bowl an Australian length (i.e. shorter than our own), the initial movement of most of their best batsmen has been back and across. This was one of the reasons for Alec's great success against them, for his fuller length, combined with his late in-swing, meant that he often wrong-footed them. He had the Don caught in his leg-trap on several occasions and it was even said – though it certainly was not true, as can be seen from the number of runs he scored against us – that the splendid Arthur Morris, a world-class opener, was Alec's 'bunny'.

'Big Al's' international career ended, rather sadly, immediately before the start of the Second Test in Sydney in 1954 because Len Hutton decided he did not fit into his tactical plan of a spearhead based on pace – Tyson and Statham, with myself as the third seamer and all-rounder. What made this decision so ironic was that the conditions for the first two days at Sydney were ideal for swing bowling and tailor-made for Alec. England, having been put in by Arthur Morris, were shot out for 154, and the ball was still moving around in the air to such an extent when the Australians went in that I concentrated on swerve rather than seam, which was unusual for me. Opening the bowling, I picked up four wickets. It was a different story in their second innings. After the humidity had cleared, the speed of Tyson and Statham saw us home, despite a truly masterful 92 not out by Neil Harvey. I have always believed that if Alec had been selected, he would have captured at least six wickets in the Australian first innings. He was such a devastating bowler in those conditions. We would have won the game, he would obviously have kept his place for the Third Test, and we could well have lost the series. – T.E.B.

Les Jackson

Fate can play cruel tricks on a man during his career, and this was very true of Les Jackson of Derbyshire; one of the finest fast bowlers I ever saw. In my opinion he was the best six-days-a-week, day-in-and-day-out paceman in county cricket since the war. Why he played only twice for England will remain a mystery which nobody can – or will – answer. There are theories and ideas, but there is no proof.

Les Jackson was that rare type of bowler who got so close to the stumps with his left foot that his right arm came over the top of them. This meant that he was actually bowling wicket to wicket. It has been said that some people did not like his action, but to me it was nearly perfect. My only complaint was that when Yorkshire were batting against Derbyshire, our batsmen found it difficult to stand properly because the heels of their boots would slip into the deep hole Les had dug with his left foot.

Many was the time that players from other counties said to me, 'It's going to be a right ten days. We're going north to Yorkshire, Lancashire and Derbyshire. It's bad enough having to bat against you and Brian, but after that we have to face Les Jackson.'

I have enquired many times why Les did not play for England as often as he should have, but I never got a satisfactory answer. Len Hutton reckoned that he was a great bowler and so did his England partner, Cyril Washbrook. Indeed, this was the view of all the players in county cricket, yet Les will never be seen as such in the Test record books, even though a whole legion of bowlers who could not lace his boots are there. It is an illustration of the unfairness which can, on occasions, occur in cricket.

I remember playing in a charity match with Les after he had retired. Ted Dexter came up to me after his innings and said, with genuine appreciation, 'I've just batted against Les Jackson, and out there it's like a little box where he's pitched the ball'. – F.S.T.

When we were drawing up our list of great seam bowlers, I was not surprised when Fred suggested the inclusion of Les Jackson, despite the fact that, in a long career, he was only twice selected for England. What makes this even more remarkable is that before the arrival of Fred, Brian, Frank, Peter and company, there was a real shortage of good pace bowlers in the country. Although his lack of recognition at international level will always remain a mystery, to understand the Les Jackson story it is necessary to examine carefully his county, Derbyshire, which proved to be both a help and a handicap.

Kent has a tradition for producing wicket-keepers, Yorkshire slow left-armers, Essex leg-spinners, Sussex brothers and cousins. And when I think of Derbyshire, a picture comes into my mind of a hard, well-polished cricket ball with an ultra-large seam, a green wicket, and an abundance of quality, just-short-of-a-length pace bowling that made run-getting a difficult and frequently painful exercise. To me, the typical Derbyshire seamer is a large, raw-boned, rather taciturn man who trundles away relentlessly and accurately, a miserly bowler who begrudges every run. But this inborn hatred of having runs scored off him can, particularly in Test cricket, prove a weakness, because a fuller length will usually bring wickets more quickly, even though it will cost more runs. Surely this is one of the main reasons why Mike Hendrick, who until recently was the county's leading seamer, never captured five wickets in an innings in 30 Tests.

The list of Derbyshire new-ball bowlers since the war is, to say the least, impressive. It includes Bill Copson, George Pope, Cliff Gladwin, Les Jackson, Harold Rhodes, Alan Ward, Mike Hendrick and now Paul Newman, who could well be competing for an England place before long. The fact that Derbyshire have had such an abundance of them has possibly led to their being taken for granted somewhat. There can be no doubt, though, that Derbyshire pacemen have generally been assisted, and made the more dangerous, by the support which has always been available, and also by their pitches which, particularly in the forties, fifties and sixties, were receptive to seam bowling. Certainly it has been far easier for pacemen to take wickets in Derbyshire than, shall we say, at Edgbaston or in Kent, and this was something the Selectors had to take into account. Being a very successful batsman or bowler in county cricket does not always make a player a sure prospect for a Test match.

The Derbyshire player with international aspirations also faced another disadvantage. He did not play for a fashionable county and therefore did not receive the same media attention as a cricketer with Middlesex or Yorkshire. This was even truer when there was only one honour being contested by the seventeen clubs, instead of the four which are up for grabs today. It can be argued, of course, that Selectors should not be influenced by the media, but they are human. Therefore, if they are constantly reading or hearing about a player, they will go and have a look at him, which is the first step towards eventual selection.

Before dealing with Les Jackson, it is worthwhile examining the record of his predecessor with the Derbyshire new ball, Bill Copson. They were, in so many ways, the same, having a short run-up, slightly round-arm, slinging body action, natural out-swing and 'nip-backer' – and a mining background. Bill was at his best before the war, when his 140 wickets in 1936 were a major reason for his county, much to everyone's surprise, winning the Championship, but he was still a formidable opponent in the forties. I opened for Essex against Bill at Valentines Park, Ilford, in my first county match, and that may be one of the reasons why he left such a lasting impression. He seemed to have unusually long arms, which combined with his reddish patch of hair and lined face made him look the type of person you would want on your side in a bar-room brawl. Later, when Bill became an umpire, I discovered that beneath that rather craggy exterior was a very jovial individual.

Although by 1946 his pace was fast-medium, rather than fast, it was easy to understand why so many who had faced him before the war reckoned that he was an even more formidable bowler than Les. I suspect, too, that he was a shade faster, and I am by no means certain that he should not have been included in this book in his own right, rather than as an appendage to Les. He was, without question, a very fine fast bowler in a period in which his contemporaries, and rivals, numbered Farnes, Voce, Gover, Allen, Nichols and 'Nobby' Clark.

The similarity in the bowling of Bill and Les is further reflected in their career records, provided one takes into account that the former missed five years when he was at his peak (and could reasonably have been expected to pick up another 600 victims), and in their treatment by the England Selectors. Bill took 1,094 wickets at a cost of 18.96 and played in three Tests, while Les secured 1,733 wickets at a cost of 17.36 and made two Test appearances. The tighter field-placings post-war would more than account for the slight difference in the cost per wicket.

Les Jackson was fortunate to have the redoubtable Cliff Gladwin as his new-ball partner at the start of his career. They comple-

Les Jackson at the start of his follow-through. His left foot, which came down with regularity in front of the middle and leg stumps, has already started to swivel.

mented each other perfectly and formed possibly the most effective English opening pair in post-war county cricket. Cliff, a tall, strong man with a very high action, bowled in-swingers which dipped in late. Originally his pace was a sharp fast-medium, but he was at his best at a lively medium with the wicket-keeper usually standing back. He added a most effective leg-cutter to his extensive repertoire and his control was exceptional. He detested conceding a run, let alone a boundary. At any time in an innings he could tell you not only the number of wickets he had taken, the number of overs bowled, the maidens and the runs scored off him, but also, in considerable detail, just how lucky the batsmen had been. A craftsman and a perfectionist, he was deadly on a green-top and a master of shutting up the game when the pitch was plumb. It was interesting to note that the introduction of the new Law allowing only two fieldsmen behind the wicket on the leg side made little difference to his effectiveness.

While Cliff wheeled away at one end, bowling his in-swingers to an attendant gaggle of short-legs, at the other end there was the menace and hostility of Les. Unlike many bowlers of his style, who stray off target whenever their timing is slightly off, Les personified accuracy. He had grooved his action so perfectly that ball after ball hit almost the same spot, something which I can verify from personal experience as I spent many hours batting against him.

Fred has already mentioned that Les bowled wicket to wicket, with his left foot coming down in front of the stumps, and this was one of the reasons why he could seam the odd ball away from the bat, as distinct from swinging it. As Fred also mentioned, I too found the place that Les landed provided me with a problem when batting, but it also troubled me when I was bowling. Apart from Jack Flavell, after he had cut down his pace and run-up, Les was the only person who dug a pit in almost the same place as I did.

The following incident illustrates the difficulty that the Derbyshire pair's accuracy, combined with their ability to exploit favourable conditions, provided for opposing batsmen. In 1957, incidently Jackson's Benefit year, I captained Essex against Derbyshire because Doug Insole was on duty with MCC, and as Dickie Dodds was also unavailable it was necessary to bring in some young players. One of these, Graham Horrex, an amateur who had been scoring heavily in club cricket, was given the experience of opening for Essex against Les and Cliff on a green-top at Buxton. By sheer determination, allied to some good fortune in that their normally safe close-fielders put him down on a few occasions, he managed to exist – that is probably the most accurate description – for over an hour. He also scored 20 runs, greatly helped by three boundaries off the edge, which as we were shot out for 80 put him in the millionaire class. When Graham returned to the pavilion, he told us that he could not understand why, for the whole time he was out in the middle, he never received anything vaguely resembling a long-hop, half-volley or full toss. All he got was a succession of deliveries which either did too much and beat the bat or which he just managed to keep out. It was, he confessed, a different game from the one he knew.

Les was never really fast, in the Larwood or Lillee sense, but he was quick enough to be distinctly unpleasant. When he was in his prime, his bouncer was more often ducked than hooked. Despite his comparatively low arm because of his slinging-style action, he could still achieve a surprising amount of lift, and he had the knack of bringing the odd one back from just short of a length into the batsman's ribs. His economical run-up, plus his physical strength, enabled 'Big Les' to keep going for long spells without any loss of his pace. He thumped the last ball of the day into the pitch with the same unemotional venom as he had the first of the morning.

There was a clinical efficiency about his bowling, which made him less exciting to watch than many less effective, but visually more exciting, bowlers, and this could have been another reason why the Selectors ignored his obvious claims. Yet year after year Les would be found close to the top of the first-class averages, with the result that he had the rare distinction of becoming something of a legend in his own playing career. Whenever I found myself batting on a green-top, and we had more than our quota in Essex, it was odds-on that one of the opposition would come up and say to me, 'I'm glad I'm not facing "Big Les" on this'. There have been faster bowlers, but none was more feared on a helpful pitch. Even on a good batting track, a long innings against Les was sure to produce a bruised right hand, as well as a few mementoes on the inside of the right thigh.

That Les Jackson was only twice chosen for England and never selected for an overseas tour remains as incomprehensible to me as it does to Fred. There was a theory that he would have been less effective on the plumb wickets overseas, but they might at least have given him one opportunity to refute it. I have sometimes wondered whether the fact that Bill Copson failed to be picked for any of the Tests when he went to Australia in 1936-37 may have had something to do with it – though it should be added that he finished at the top of the tour bowling averages. Their methods were so similar.

I can still remember clearly the faces and the view of Les's colleagues when it was announced that the last place on the boat to Australia in 1950 had gone to John Warr, who was not in the same class. Essex were playing Derbyshire at Southchurch Park and I spent the evening with their side. They simply could not understand how he could have been ignored, though not by so much as a word or a gesture did 'Big Les' suggest his disappointment. He simply sat downing his ale from a straight pint glass with the same impressive efficiency that was the hallmark of his bowling. – T.E.B.

Brian Statham

The majority of fast bowlers have, like world-class boxers, an aggressive streak. This provides them with the extra devil to battle on when the runs are flowing or on placid pitches. Many regard their bouncer as a weapon for literally blasting out the opposition, while some take their dislike of opposing batsmen to extremes and show a lack of self-control. This tendency is, sadly, on the increase and has provoked several unpleasant incidents. There was, for instance, John Snow's shoulder-charge on the diminutive Gavaskar at Lord's in 1971, Croft's crashing into a New Zealand umpire and Holding's kicking down of the stumps in that same series. Dennis Lillee, well known for his colourful, if somewhat limited, vocabulary, added physical abuse to his vocal misdemeanours when he kicked Javed Miandad in a Test match in Australia. For this behaviour, which offended the spirit of cricket, he was fined a derisory £100 by his colleagues and later banned from a couple of one-day internationals by the Australian Board of Control.

If Dennis had behaved in this fashion in another era, he would, in all probability, never have been selected for his country again. But then it would never have happened in the first place. Can you imagine Ray Lindwall kicking a batsman? Times have changed, but, in this context, not for the better.

In complete contrast to the majority of members of the fast bowlers' brigade, Brian Statham was essentially an easy-going individual who seldom allowed himself to become ruffled. Even when a couple of chances had been spilled, he would carry on bowling without any noticeable change of expression. If he beat the bat a few times without getting a touch, he might give a rueful chuckle, or make some comment like, 'It doesn't seem to be my day'. He never indulged in extravagant gestures, bad language or gnashing of teeth. His behaviour was at all times civilised.

His bowling philosophy was simple but also effective. It was based on the principle that if a batsman missed the ball, it would hit the stumps. Whatever the pitch, the country, or the situation, he followed this basic formula with enormous success.

My first encounter with Brian came when he was flown out to Australia with Roy Tattersall following injuries to Doug Wright

Brian Statham moves into his delivery stride. Notice that he is
looking round his left arm, which was why he tended to move the
ball into the batsman, and his cocked right wrist.

(badly torn muscle) and myself (broken thumb) during the 1950-51 tour. I met them off the plane in Sydney and spent the evening with them before they flew on to join the side in Adelaide. At the time it seemed strange to me that Brian should be there, for I had scarcely heard of him and had never seen him play. That he should have gained preference over such bowlers as Les Jackson or a young Yorkshire quickie called Trueman, who was beginning to make a name for himself, was both puzzling and amazing. Nor, as we drank the first of what, over the years, were to be numerous glasses of lager, did he look the part. He seemed too slight, too young and too shy to make much of an impression in Australia. But I was very wrong.

At that time Brian's pace was fast-medium, rather than fast, but he impressed everybody with his accuracy. It was obvious that, when he filled out and gained those extra yards of pace, he would be a most formidable and mean – in the bowling sense – fast bowler. He had an easy, bounding approach which provided him with the ideal impetus for his high, whippy, if slightly open-chested, action, while he was deceptively wiry and much tougher than he appeared.

Bowlers are always more effective when they can team up with a class but contrasting partner at the other end. Brian, for much of his international career, shared the new ball with Fred Trueman, and together they were a world-class pair; possibly the finest England has ever produced. For a short period, too, he was a vital part of a memorable match-winning partnership with Frank Tyson.

How did Brian compare with Fred? For a start, he had greater accuracy and control, whereas Fred was more volatile, did more with the ball, was a shade faster and produced a higher percentage of unplayable deliveries. Personally I preferred facing Fred, for the simple reason that I could never see when, or where, I was ever going to score a run off Brian. He was the type of bowler who considered one half-volley a match to be over-generous. Ball after ball would pitch just short of a length on, or just fractionally outside, the off stump, interspersed with an occasional yorker, especially at the start of an innings. At least Fred was likely to send down the occasional half-volley. In contrast, class batsmen like Tom Graveney and Colin Cowdrey preferred facing Brian because they knew where the ball would be. Fred, being more unpredictable, was more likely to produce the ball which moves very late and requires a very good player to touch. Tom and Colin were that good, and paid for their class with the edge that a lesser player would have missed.

For a captain, Brian was a dream; a genuine fast bowler who was not temperamental, was fully dependable, very economical and was prepared to bowl up the hill or into the wind without complaint. He made an ideal tourist, liked and respected by both his colleagues and the opposition and possessing a sense of humour and proportion so invaluable when things are going wrong on tour and the moaning has begun. He quietly enjoyed a party, especially those at which, very late in the proceedings, he could remove his shoes, take over the kitchen, and toss an excellent pancake.

Like most of his generation, Brian kept fit by bowling rather than by training in order to be fit to bowl. Blessed with the stamina and the physique of a marathon runner, he could not only sustain his pace for long spells but also, more important, he was able to come back at the end of a long day in the field for a final burst. Such attributes, combined with his accommodating nature, meant that there was a temptation to over-bowl him; to give him that one extra over which somehow turned into six.

Fortunately, he usually recovered quickly from such treatment with no ill effects, although his effort in the 1955 Lord's Test did leave its mark. Called on to bowl throughout the South African second innings, he responded by taking seven for 39 in 29 overs to bring England victory by 71 runs. But the cost was high. It was nearly twelve months before he was back to his peak. However, it was not so much the strain of sending down 29 consecutive overs that did the damage, but the fact that he had already bowled 27 overs in the first innings, while in the previous match for his county he had bowled 52 overs, his normal stint *whether he was taking wickets or not.* – T.E.B.

 Brian Statham came into first-class cricket in 1950 after he had completed his RAF service, and his success was immediate. Although he had played in only fourteen matches for Lancashire, capturing 36 wickets, when England ran into trouble with injuries in Australia in 1950-51 he was flown out as a replacement. His selection owed much to Cyril Washbrook, and to a remarkable opening spell in his first Roses Match in which he had bowled Lowson, Lester and Watson for 'ducks' and later picked up a further two wickets after a recovery. Both spells had also been carefully noted by Len Hutton, Cyril's opening partner in the

England team, and without the support of this influential pair he would never have arrived on the international scene quite so quickly.

There is no doubt that Brian was the most accurate quick bowler who has ever played cricket. In practice, he was actually a fast bowler with the control of a medium-pacer. He believed that if the batsman played and missed, he should hit the stumps. This, of course, did not always happen, for he would often beat the outside edge with the ball that went straight on. Which is one of the reasons why he was inclined to be labelled an unlucky bowler.

When younger, Brian was a useful soccer player, and I understand that the Wolves were interested in signing him when he was in the forces. He was, in fact, recommended to Lancashire by a corporal in the RAF, and had this not happened I wonder if he would have slipped through his county's net and, like Frank Tyson, gone to play for another club.

Essentially an honest, hard-working bowler, Brian played cricket the right way, keen to win and hating to lose. Although he was thought of both in and outside the game by people who did not know him as a quiet man, this was not really true. He was witty and had the knack of coming back with dry quips that would have people doubled up with laughter. I spent many hours with him on planes, trains, and boats, in pavilions, at parties, in nets, in hotels, and I often shared a room with him on tour. The two weeks we roomed together on the 1959-60 tour to the West Indies are among the most hilarious of my life.

On one occasion after a typically late Saturday night, which we normally had after a week's cricket, we took advantage of a lengthy lie-in on the Sunday morning. Eventually we both woke up, had a cup of coffee, and when Brian lit the inevitable cigarette we started to natter. We talked about home, cricket, the current Test and a host of other things. Further pots of coffee were ordered and consumed while we carried on chatting, until eventually Brian said, 'Don't you think it's about time we got up and went downstairs?' I agreed, but when I pulled back the curtains we were both amazed to find it was already dark. We had talked the day away, even though neither of us could remember the exact details of the topics we had covered.

That evening we went with some of the other lads to the cinema, to see a Western. Films were one of our favourite forms of relaxation. We all sat in the front row of the balcony, with Brian, or

George as he was usually known, sitting at the end. When an usherette came to our row and asked whether we wanted an ice cream or chocolates, George gave his infectious chuckle and said 'A beer would be better'. The girl laughed and went away, but she was back inside ten minutes with a tray of canned lager. Only George could have managed that and, having paid for the drinks, he put in a repeat order for about fifteen minutes' time. Which we also got.

People are always asking how Brian Statham came to be known as 'George'. As a start, because he was slim and did not have the build normally associated with a fast bowler, he acquired the not inappropriate nickname of 'Greyhound'. However, when the Lancashire opening batsman, Winston Place, who was known as George, retired, Brian is said to have sat on the bench in the dressing-room, smoking that inevitable cigarette, and announced, 'We have to have a George, and from now on that's my name'. Apparently, though I don't know why, there has always been a George in the Lancashire side. And even if it isn't the right reason why Brian was George, it is a lovely, typically Statham story.

Having double-jointed shoulders meant that Brian had several amusing little party pieces, like skipping through his arms or putting his arms behind his back and scratching both ears. It was always fun seeing him remove his sweater, for he would put his arm down his back, take hold of the bottom of the sweater and pull it over his head.

Brian was an ideal model for any young fast bowler. He had a fluent, athletic run-up that was rounded off by a good action, even if he bowled on the inside of his left elbow and was slightly chest on. His main point of attack was the off stump, or just outside, and he would tend to bring the ball back in off the seam. He rarely swung the ball in the air; in fact, he told me that on the odd occasion when he did find himself swinging the ball in a match, he could not control it. This, for a bowler of such exceptional accuracy, was very odd, but when it happened, all Brian could do was take his sweater and come off because he simply was not able to bowl at the stumps. Nor did he ever understand why he would suddenly find himself swinging the ball away. In matches Brian did not drag his right foot, yet in the nets he not only tended to drag but also often made the ball swerve. Again, he did not know why.

Although he did not use it very often, Brian possessed a particularly nasty bouncer. This was somewhat surprising because he did not achieve as much lift off a length as many other fast bowlers. Rather, his action tended to make the ball skid on into the batsman, which is why, on a slow pitch, I rate him as possibly the best of all fast bowlers. On the slowest of wickets he had the ability of sliding the ball into you more quickly than anybody else of his speed. What made Brian's bouncer so difficult to negotiate was that it was both lower and flatter than most, and it tended to follow the batsman.

One of the best he ever bowled was during the 1959-60 tour to the Caribbean, in the Test at Sabina Park. Yet strangely I never saw him bowl worse than he did in that match. For once he simply could not find his line or length. He went off and changed his boots, in fact did everything to rediscover his rhythm, but it was one of those rare days when nothing goes right. If you are a bowler and ever feel like giving up the game, take heart and remember what once happened to that most reliable of all quickies.

In the last over before lunch at Sabina I slipped in a short one to Easton McMorris, who fended it off with his glove to Mike Smith at short-leg and we all started to walk off for lunch – apart from the batsman. Eventually we appealed, only for the umpire to give him not out. We were all furious and I was livid. And it hardly pleased us when, during the interval, the West Indian captain asked Peter May if it was all right for another player to come in as McMorris had gone for an X-ray on the hand where I'd hit him. Peter agreed, but in the event McMorris got back from the hospital in time to continue his innings. Everybody knew that I was going after him, including McMorris, who had an idea that I was not too pleased and managed to stay away from my end. Eventually, though, Brian came on at the other. Everyone had forgotten him, especially as he had been well below his best during the morning. Now he limbered up, came in like an express, and let go that low, skidding bouncer because, like all fast bowlers, he was not partial to batsmen who stand there when they are out. The ball hit McMorris in the chest with a thud that could be heard all round the ground, felled him and forced him to leave the field as he kept getting blood in his mouth. Brian may be remembered as the quiet man, but when roused he could be as nasty as anyone.

I was both lucky and delighted to play with Brian in so many Tests and to form a new-ball partnership with him. It made life so much easier to have someone like him at the other end, and not having to do most of the hard work yourself was something he could appreciate too. We both of us often had to do that in county cricket when there was only an ordinary seamer in support. What made our partnership even better was that we complemented each other because our styles were entirely different. We were rather like a left-arm and a right-arm spinning partnership. I predominantly swung the ball away from the right-hander, like the left-arm spinner, while Brian seamed it into him, like the off-spinner. This played a major part in our success. – F.S.T.

Fred Trueman

As with most young fast bowlers, my ambition was to be the fastest in the world. The outcome was that in my early days with Yorkshire I tried to bowl too fast, lost my rhythm and became very erratic. But there were two other reasons for my wildness. From time to time I would get my run-up wrong, with the result that either I would arrive at the stumps too soon or find myself struggling to get there. Consequently my timing at the moment of delivery was not quite right. I also found that I could not control my natural away-swing. There were many occasions when I would run up, aim at the off stump, and find the ball swerve away and miss both bat and stumps by a long long way. I would then be told, quite correctly, that I was wasting the new ball. The trouble was that when I tried to switch to the leg stump, the ball often would not swing but would carry straight on to miss the leg stump. This also was a waste of the new ball, and as often as not it gave the batsman a free hit to leg, where there were few fieldsmen.

I reckon it took me six or seven years, from the time I first played for Yorkshire, to learn my chosen trade and I think the turning-point was in a 1953 Services Match at Lord's. My captain was Alan Shirreff, who gained a pre-war Blue for Cambridge and played a certain amount of county cricket as a medium-paced bowler for several counties. That day he was on a hat-trick. Up until then I had been regarded purely as an outfielder with a reliable pair of hands and a powerful throw that was not always as accurate as the 'keeper, or my team-mates, would have liked. Alan called me up to join the short-legs, and after I had held the catch which gave him his hat-trick, he told me, 'If you can catch like that at short-leg, you can stay there'. Later he suggested to my county that this was an ideal position for me, and so I found myself being stationed regularly at leg-slip.

In this position you have to watch the batsman, and I began to study how they stood, their grip, stance, initial movement, whether they were mainly off- or on-side players, their weaknesses and their strengths. Not only did I find this fascinating in itself, but the knowledge stored away in my memory bank proved invaluable to me when I had to bowl against them. For example, I would know

Fred Trueman, about to come into his delivery stride, is beautifully balanced, his head is steady and eyes looking over his left shoulder. His right foot has been grounded so far behind the bowling crease because of his drag.

to attack from the outset the middle and leg stumps of a pronounced off-side player. Conversely, against the strong on-side player I would try to get even closer to the stumps at my end, aim at his off stump and try to move the ball away. I also knew the batsman who was frightened by pace and would normally drop him one early on. I have always believed the bouncer to be a useful weapon in the armoury of a fast bowler, but it can be, and often is, over-used. Guilty of doing this in my early days, later I could see little point in bowling bouncers against a batsman who did not hook and was an expert ducker, against one who was a really good hooker, once he was well settled, or against the tailenders. The latter I felt I should be able to bowl out. The answer to nine, ten, jack is surely a fast ball which hits them on the thigh if they fail to make contact, followed by a yorker, leg stump.

Because I was always trying to swing the ball, I believe I bowled a fuller length than most of the present generation of pace bowlers, with two exceptions – Lillee and Botham. You cannot swing the ball if you bowl too short, and though the swinging half-volley will often be hit to the boundary, it is also a great wicket-taker.

From the outset I found that, from time to time and for no apparent reason, I would bowl a ball which would pitch outside the off stump and come back to hit the middle, the 'nip-backer'. Later I learnt to bowl it deliberately by dropping my right arm slightly, and I also learnt how to bowl cutters off a shorter run at fast-medium. Because I was a natural out-swing bowler, as a result of my body action, it took me a long time to learn how to bowl the in-swinger by opening out my left shoulder early and seaming the ball into the right-hand batsman.

I still maintain that bowling at a batsman is a game within a game, a battle of wits. You try to dominate him and make him play the shots you want him to play, while he is attempting to dominate you. My aim was to try to wrong-foot the batsman. If I succeeded, there was always the chance of a wicket, because one mistake by him can be fatal. On the other hand a bowler can, and will, send down indifferent deliveries that go unpunished and sometimes even get him a wicket.

There have been many occasions when I have bowled really well and finished with nought for plenty, while another time I have bowled badly and ended up with six wickets for 20. But that is exactly what cricket is all about. Over the years, though, luck will even itself out and the bowler who thinks will not only reap a much bigger harvest of wickets than one who does not, but also he will enjoy his work so much more.

People often ask me to name the greatest batsman I have seen. My answer is Len Hutton. Although there have been better hookers, stronger drivers off the back foot, harder hitters and more spectacular strokemakers, Len was easily the finest player on all wickets. He was a master craftsman. I've watched him make runs on a 'sticky', a 'green-top', a 'road', fast pitches, slow pitches and feather-beds. In addition to scoring thousands of runs, breaking countless records and possessing a fine temperament, a marvellous defence and a glorious cover-drive, Len was, unlike Geoff Boycott for example, always entertaining to watch at the crease, even when runs were coming slowly. His technique was not only near perfection, but also it was elegant.

Which batsmen hooked my bouncers the best? I have had to divide them into two categories, those I bowled against in my early days, when I was at my fastest, and those I bowled against in my prime, when I was fractionally slower and used it more sparingly. In the first category I would place Cyril Washbrook, who may have holed out on the boundary from time to time but scored a great many runs with the hook, Denis Compton and two very quick-footed little men, Everton Weekes and Bill Edrich. In the second category come Peter Burge, strong and brutal, Bill Lawry, practical and efficient, and Gary Sobers, who was magic.

Of all the many batsmen I bowled against, the most aggravating was 'Slasher' Mackay, because his judgement of what he could safely leave was so exceptional. Unlike most batsmen, and left-handers in particular, he knew exactly where his off stump was and would confidently ignore a delivery which was only an inch off target. The combination of his judgement, patience and ability to steer balls down through little gaps made bowling at him both difficult and infuriating.

The best player of fast bowling on good wickets was Reg Simpson, a tall, graceful opening batsman. His method was simple and made bowling bouncers at him a complete waste of time because he did not hook. His initial movement was back and across his stumps, and if the ball rose above waist high he swayed backwards or forwards so that it passed harmlessly one side or the other.

Who were the batsmen I most feared when bowling against them for Yorkshire because they had the ability, if things went well, to collar an accurate attack? The first was undoubtedly Denis

Compton, who was so good that when he was in the mood it was difficult to know exactly where to bowl at him. Roy Marshall was a superb cutter and an exciting destroyer of opposing attacks, while I was always especially grateful to see the back of the diminutive George Emmett.

The most devastating batsman I encountered in Test cricket was Gary Sobers. Once he had settled himself in, he had the ability to hit the really good ball to the boundary with a perfectly straight bat. The two most devastating players at the present time are Viv Richards and Ian Botham. Although it is possible to criticise Viv for being too on-side conscious, he can drive superbly through the covers, as he once demonstrated against the luckless Bob Willis at Old Trafford, and he does hit the ball exceptionally hard. Ian is a law unto himself, the nearest thing to a high-class hitter, not slogger, I have even seen. – F.S.T.

It is doubtful whether anybody has had the distinction of batting against Fred Trueman in first-class cricket more often than I. In addition to playing for Essex against Yorkshire for two decades, I regularly found myself facing him each summer in two Scarborough Festival matches, as well as a host of Gentlemen v Players fixtures. I even opened the batting against him in one of those rather pointless Test Trials. And as I often played for England and went on several tours with him – even captained him on a number of occasions – I can justifiably claim a greater knowledge of Fred's bowling than most. In addition, as he has been a close friend for some thirty years, more than ten of them as colleagues on Test Match Special, I can also claim to know the man, not just the living legend.

My first memories are of Fred as a young, extremely aggressive, volatile, tearaway fast bowler, who was a little lacking in control, both as a bowler and as a person. There was, however, no disguising his superb body action and that strong, rather bull-like physique which made you think you'd want him on your side in a free-for-all. These qualities, moreover, indicated that he was destined to become one of the game's immortals. His temperament drew spectators' attention towards him. The action and the build ensured that he would last longer and not break down as often as most other members of his trade.

When Fred made his début for England against India in 1952, he utterly destroyed them with his pace, immediately becoming not just another exciting fast bowler but also a personality who made news and captured headlines. There have been few more stimulating sights on the cricket field since the war than Fred Trueman on the warpath. He had everything: the beautiful run-up, side-on body action and controlled follow-through; the flowing black mane, the ferocious scowl and a range of extravagant gestures; controversy and colour; bouncers, flying stumps and full-length catches in the slips; disciplined force combined with primitive strength. Enveloping him was the drama that comes when a great artist is on stage.

Throughout his Yorkshire career, Fred was handicapped by seldom having sufficient support at the other end with the new ball. This resulted in his often being over-bowled, although he was fortunate that his county's spin attack was stronger than that of most other counties. Nevertheless, with tour matches and Test appearances also taken into account, he would expect to send down more than 1,000 overs and take well in excess of 100 wickets a year. That he did this year after year underlies his physique and stamina, as well as his ability.

As with good wine, Fred improved with age. He lost some of his speed through the air, but his control of line, length and movement improved. He began to think out, as well as blast out, the opposition. In his early days he gave the impression that he believed he could remove any player, irrespective of his ability, or the state of the pitch, by sheer pace. And he tended to overdo the bouncer, which reduced its effectiveness. However, in the early fifties he was without question very fast, quick enough to terrify the timid and unsettle the brave. Only Frank Tyson was, for a brief period, quicker, but as he did not move the ball like Fred he was easier to play in England.

Fred did not reach his peak until his vintage years between 1958 and 1964. When he made his first overseas tour, to the West Indies in 1953-54, he was raw, and rather naive, so that he was not initially as successful as he probably should have been. Later he was to prove himself equally as effective on the less sympathetic pitches overseas as at home, and, it must also be stressed, against a large number of high-class batsmen. On all wickets, and in all conditions, it is doubtful whether there has been a more complete fast bowler. He had fire, aggressiveness, pace, control and ability to move the ball, allied to a glorious action, limitless confidence in his own ability and a vivid imagination.

These last two were important, because Fred Trueman was always convinced that he was capable of bowling anybody out. He also believed that he was invariably doing something with the ball. He might clean-bowl with a straight half-volley some wretched number ten who was treading on the square-leg umpire's toes. But if you made the mistake of asking Fred what happened (or even if you did not), he would hold forth on the subject at considerable length and relate in great detail how the ball had started outside off stump and dipped in very late. Even the catch which was purely and simply the result of a badly played stroke from a long-hop would end up as part of Fred's Machiavellian plot.

Fred's considerable imagination also extended to chances that were put down off his bowling, some of which no-one else would have regarded as a difficult half-chance. I shall always treasure a moment from Fred's young days when, in Jamaica early on the tour, he bowled a bouncer. The batsman played a fine hook shot which would have decapitated our wretched short-leg if he had been six inches taller. But Fred, passing me on his way back to his mark, complained bitterly that that was the fourteenth catch which had been put down so far on the trip – a matter of four matches, including the one we were playing. Needless to say, I could recall only one of them. We were rather proud of our catching on that tour and did not miss many chances.

I always enjoyed batting against fast bowlers and wrist-spinners, largely because the former employed fairly attacking fields, allowing runs to be picked up without having to hit the ball too hard, while the latter tended to be more generous than other bowlers with long-hops and full tosses. In addition, there was the exhilaration provided by the physical challenge of facing pace, which appealed to me. (I was helped by the belief, not always true, that I would not be hit.) I also noticed that quick bowlers were inclined to lose their temper quickly and become more interested in knocking me out than getting me out. Once this occurred, I reckoned that the chances of my staying at the crease had considerably improved and I had won that particular battle.

It follows, therefore, that I loved my many duels with Fred; encounters which were enlivened by the numerous asides from both of us. When I arrived at the wicket and found Fred bowling at me, my first thought was survival. I would aim to spend most of the first few overs playing half-cock off the front foot, hoping that Fred, in his efforts to york me, or have me caught behind, would bowl a full half-volley which could be pushed safely through the sparsely populated covers.

I reckon that I sensed a high percentage of his bouncers before he released them, although, as I discovered on one occasion at Leyton, this was not always a reliable indicator. Fred had not been selected to play for England against the 1965 South African tourists, and he arrived for the Essex match determined to convince everybody – not that we needed convincing – that he was still the fastest bowler in the country. The pitch was quick, with plenty of bounce, as I discovered when I walked out to bat at about ten to twelve with three of my players already back in the pavilion and one of them on his way to hospital. There was also a certain amount of blood, plus teeth, around the crease – the result of an ill-advised hook – so life for the next forty minutes was full of excitement. Just before the luncheon interval, Fred came back for a couple of overs and soon let go his bouncer, which I anticipated and ducked. Unfortunately it failed to rise as much as I had expected and hit me on the back of my head. Remembering that sound piece of boxing advice, I took a full count, which ensured there would not be time for another over and also enabled Fred to come up and say, 'Sorry Trev, old son, there are many more I'd have rather hit than thee'. I was left to wonder which particular Selector he had been thinking about when he ran up to bowl.

On a less violent note, there was one Gents v Players match when I found myself batting against Fred, with Godfrey Evans behind the stumps. I agreed to 'give Fred the charge', provided Godfrey and all the slips would join me in the shout of 'charge' just as Fred released the ball. The combination of our 'charge' in unison, the sight of me moving down the pitch, and the ball being hoicked just over mid-on was almost too much for Fred Trueman. He simply stood there, legs apart, arms upraised, saying 'What the hell's going on, Sunshine?' Or words to that effect! – T.E.B.

Frank Tyson

Whenever there is talk about fast bowling, I always say without fear of contradiction that the quickest bowler I have ever seen, or played against, was Frank Tyson. My first sight of him in action was in 1953, when Yorkshire played a pre-season practice match at a little seaside resort called Redcar. Len Hutton opened the batting for us that day with Frank Lowson, and the talk in our dressing-room after our innings went something like this.

'What did you think of that bowler at the far end, the big lad?' Len, always a very good judge of a cricketer, asked Frank and Norman Yardley.

'A bit quick; in fact very quick indeed', came back the answer from both of them.

Frank then asked me for my opinion, which I gave as best I could seeing that I didn't bat in the innings.

'From the pavilion he certainly seemed to be making one or two hurry their shots.'

Frank not only had the ability to bowl very fast, but he also had brains and had qualified as a teacher before going into first-class cricket. He was originally turned down by the county of his birth, Lancashire, and after gaining an honours degree at Durham University he joined Northamptonshire, making his début rather later than most as a professional cricketer. There were two fine Australians playing for the Midlands county when Frank joined them, George Tribe and Jock Livingstone, and before the start of Yorkshire's match with them, George asked me if I had seen Frank bowl. I told him only once, at Redcar.

'Look at my hands', he said. Both of them were badly bruised from trying to take, and taking, slip catches off Frank's bowling.

Frank was so quick that I often saw him beat a batsman when his bat was still going up on the back-stroke, which illustrates just how fast he was. Even on the Northampton wicket, which was extremely slow, the distance between Frank at the commencement of his run and wicket-keeper Keith Andrew was something like 78 yards. On a small ground, the slips were close to the boundary.

I watched Frank bowl that day at Northampton and there was no argument. He was exceptionally quick. Later I was asked what

I thought about him. 'He's the quickest thing I've ever seen', I said, 'but I don't think he'll last very long'. Immediately some eyebrows were raised. Was I trying to knock this new quickie? This, however, was certainly not my intention, as I explained.

'Frank has a very long run-up which isn't athletic. His approach is rather stiff-jointed, and his pace is derived from his very powerful shoulders and physique. When he goes into his delivery stride, he not only picks his left leg up higher than most bowlers, but he brings it down on the outside of his heel with his toe pointing towards cover. As he's over six feet tall and comes down very hard, this puts an enormous strain on his leg and ankle. It seems to me that he'll eventually injure himself.'

This, in fact, is what did occur later in his all-too-brief career.

Although Frank never took 100 wickets in a season for Northamptonshire, and surprisingly captured only 525 during his eight years with them, he was chosen for his pace and potential, rather than on his wickets, for the 1954-55 Australian tour. It turned out to be an inspired selection, because his bag of 28 wickets was the single most-important factor in England's retaining the Ashes. He formed a devastating spearhead with Brian Statham and, as a Yorkshireman, I could not help feeling glad that Lancashire had missed him. It certainly would not have been very pleasant facing both Brian and Frank in the Roses Match. They would have formed the most fearsome opening attack in county cricket since Larwood and Voce.

Although Frank, for me, will always remain the fastest bowler I have encountered, once his terrific pace had gone he had nothing to fall back on. He relied so much on sheer strength that he did not possess the basic action, body swing, and rhythm to last as long as, say, Dennis Lillee or myself. Without the breathtaking pace, he became just another bowler. Like a meteor which flashes across the sky, creating an unforgettable impression and then vanishing, so Frank burst on to the first-class cricket scene. He retired very early from the game and then emigrated to Australia where he taught in Melbourne and coached cricket, becoming the Victorian state coach. Today he writes and broadcasts on the game. – F.S.T.

Frank Tyson was the fastest bowler England has produced since the war. Just as a heavyweight boxer relies on a knockout punch for victory, Frank depended on sheer speed. He blew into county and, very quickly, Test cricket rather like the typhoon to which he

78

This picture of Frank Tyson, at the start of his pronounced toe-drag,
illustrates the enormous strain he put on his left leg, which he
raised higher than most bowlers.

was so often likened, leaving behind him a trail of destruction before swiftly disappearing from the scene.

For a few short years he was the quickest I ever played with, or against. Michael Holding and Dennis Lillee at their peak may have rivalled him for speed, and certainly were more complete bowlers, but I doubt if they were as fast through the air. Pace is always difficult to estimate, but I think this story illustrates better than anything the speed of Frank Tyson. During the 1954-55 Australian tour, when Frank was at his most devastating, I spent some time with Arthur Morris, who had the doubtful honour of opening the innings for Australia. However, he was also a world-class player, and a good judge of bowlers, so I asked Arthur how he found batting against Frank (other than frightening) and he summed it up perfectly. He reckoned that the difference in pace between Brian Statham and myself was just about the same as that between Frank and Brian! At the time Brian was a genuine fast bowler; my own pace was a lively fast-medium. So that difference was considerable.

Frank's success was due to sheer speed through the air, as was seen by the number of Australians who, in 1954-55, were bowled by straight full tosses and half-volleys which they set out to hit but in doing so failed to bring down their bats quickly enough. It will always be a mystery to me that the Australian Selectors did not choose 'Slasher' Mackay, who was such an expert at blunting pace because of his exceptional judgement of line, his small backlift and the straightness of his bat. I have a feeling, though, that they made the mistake of going for style rather than performance.

To stand in the slips with Frank operating was an experience, for despite frequently being stationed over thirty yards back, one still felt too close for comfort. I recall one occasion, in South Africa in 1956-57 when Frank was probably a shade slower than in Australia, I managed to get a full hand to an involuntary snick. It literally forced my fingers open and carried on to the boundary without allowing time for our very fine third man to move more than one pace.

When I first encountered Frank, he used a long, ugly and rather clumsy run-up. But in Australia he found he was able to generate the same speed and obtain greater control by using an abbreviated approach of under fifteen yards. This had become obvious in the nets where, off a few paces, he was much too quick for comfort. The reason was that his pace was derived from his body action, which incorporated a toe-drag, and his magnificent pair of shoulders. As with most toe-draggers, Frank's left leg bent at the moment of delivery, with the result that he did not achieve as much life as many bowlers with steeper actions who were much slower through the air. Consequently his bouncer, though very quick, had to be pitched shorter than one from, say, Thomson.

Frank's haul of wickets in England was surprisingly small for a bowler of his great pace; indeed, in terms of wickets taken, it could be said that he was fortunate to be picked for Australia. One of the main reasons was that the pitches in Northamptonshire tended to be slow, and he did not move the ball to any great extent, either in the air or off the wicket.

One of the great joys of playing county cricket was meeting in the opposing side someone with whom you had shared the ups and downs of an overseas tour. It certainly increased my pleasure whenever Essex played Northamptonshire and I found myself facing Frank. Quite apart from the obvious challenge and excitement of batting against the fastest bowler in the world, there was the fun of the inter-over chat show. Frank would suggest it was about time I produced my other shot, and following questions about our respective social lives, I would enquire when he was going to start slipping himself.

One moment I particularly treasure was when Essex met Northants on a distinctly lively pitch in Chalkwell Park. Dickie Dodds took seven off Frank's first over – a top-edged six via the short third-man boundary and an involuntary but welcome single. From then on, at the other end, Dickie proceeded to play a series of fine drives on the up off a medium-pacer while Gordon Barker weaved and ducked against Frank. And with some 40 runs on the board from our opening pair, Gordon had still not got off the mark. So he went down the pitch and asked Dickie, a devout Christian and a member of MRA, if he would have a word with the Almighty and ask Him to shine a little divine light down his end.

Injury and his decision to settle in Australia made Frank's first-class career all too brief. He was a lively companion with a good brain and a fine tourist, so it was no surprise that he did well 'down under'. At least a decade after he had retired from first-class cricket I had the pleasure of fielding in the slips to him again in a Rothmans Cavaliers match, and though he had reduced his run still further, he was appreciably quicker than most of the county pacemen at that time. – T.E.B.

John Snow immediately after he has released the ball.
Notice the splendid position of his head and how high
his left arm has swung behind him.

John Snow

It has often been said that one of the essential requisites of a fast bowler is a broad backside, but the truth is that they come in all sizes and shapes. For this generalisation certainly did not apply to John Snow, who was built on the lines of the fictional cowboy hero – six feet one, rangy and narrow at the hips with a small backside accentuated by the trendy, tight trousers he wore. His temperament when bowling was also in keeping with the 'spaghetti western' anti-hero – mean, moody and essentially a loner who was permanently at odds with the establishment, sometimes with, but often without, cause.

John made his international début for England against New Zealand at Lord's in 1965, and he went on to play 49 Tests in which he captured 202 wickets. He took five or more wickets in an innings on no fewer than eight occasions to justify his claim to be regarded as one of the finest of England's post-war fast bowlers, even though throughout his international career he suffered from not having a partner of the same calibre at the other end. In 1970-71, he played a major part in England winning the Ashes in Australia, picking up 31 victims in six Tests, including a decisive seven for 40 in the Fourth Test at Sydney. This match was also notable for the début of Bob Willis, who was eventually to become Snow's successor, and for Bill Lawry's carrying his bat (for 60 not out) in the Australian second innings.

It was in the closing stages of this tour that John was warned, quite unfairly in my opinion, by umpire Rowan after Terry Jenner was hit on the face in Australia's first innings of the final Test. Although he had employed the bumper to good effect in the earlier Tests, largely because so many of the Australians had played it badly, Stackpole being one of the few exceptions, he did not bowl it particularly well at Sydney. Far too many balls flew harmlessly over the batsman's head. I was sitting with a party which I had taken from England to see the Tests and had been complaining about John's waste of energy when, with the second new ball, he found the right height and direction and suddenly let one go at the luckless Jenner. It was a beautiful bouncer. In that particular spell John certainly could not have been accused of persistently bowling bouncers, and even though Jenner was a tailender, he was also the Australian number nine, had been in for some time, and the Ashes were at stake.

The outcome was all too predictable. John reacted angrily to the warning, and his captain, Ray Illingworth, was also, understandably, incensed. A small portion of the Sydney crowd, not the most restrained in the world, barracked, a few empty beer cans were thrown at John as he made his way down to the fine-leg boundary, and a spectator grabbed his shirt. To the astonishment of all, Ray led his side off the field as a protest at the beer cans and it was some time before play restarted – a classic example of over-reaction by all concerned.

Unquestionably John's finest tour was to the West Indies, under Colin Cowdrey, in 1967-68 when he took 27 wickets at 18.66 apiece in just four Tests, as many as any England bowler had taken in a full series in the West Indies. He did not play in the First Test. What makes his figures so especially remarkable is that they were obtained on very good batting pitches against a powerful batting line-up in a series in which every Test would have been drawn had Gary Sobers not chosen to make a gallant, if somewhat quixotic, declaration in Trinidad.

Although John Snow first went to Sussex as a batsman, it soon became obvious that the county had a fast bowler with more potential than any since Maurice Tate. I first faced him in his early days with Sussex, when he was keen to bowl – not always the case later in his career – and I liked what I saw. Although the pitch was soft and on the slow side, from a short, beautifully relaxed run-up John was able to make the ball lift steeply and bring the odd one back sharply off the seam. He came down hard on a braced left leg with a fine, high, rocking action. Timing was all important in his action as it was largely responsible for both his pace and his control.

In general, I think it could be said that John was a much better bowler for England than for Sussex because he relished the extra challenge of the big occasion and the large crowd. There were times when he gave the impression that he was bored with the county game, an attitude which I found a little strange as there are many worse ways of earning a living than playing professional cricket. But in full cry, John Snow bowling was one of the finest sights in cricket: genuine pace, a brooding hostility, and that lovely flowing action. – T.E.B.

It was in 1964 when Ted Dexter told me he had a young fast bowler down at Sussex whom he believed should do well and I took my first look at John in action. I was immediately impressed. He was quicker than he looked, used a short, brisk run-up, and his bowling arm came over fast and high so that batsmen found they were frequently having their knuckles rapped. He had a vicious bouncer and clearly did not mind against whom he used it, which was not true of a number of fast bowlers. They might be only too happy to dish out the bouncers, but they were careful not to upset anybody who was able to retaliate. Today it's a different story, and the first ball from a fast bowler at another is often a bouncer, whereas in my day it was a yorker, leg stump.

Because initially he tended to bowl too short, it took John some time to realise his full potential. He became a world-class bowler when he started to bowl a slightly fuller length, and, though he had neither the backside nor the broad shoulders I used to think of as essentials for fast bowling, he will go down as one of the best England has produced. Ray Illingworth told me that he had never seen any England paceman seam the ball as much in Australia as 'Snowy' did in 1970-71, when Ray was skippering the England team which won the Ashes.

Like most fast bowlers, John had a volatile temperament and fire in his belly. Additionally he was decidedly unpredictable. Nobody could be sure what his reaction would be to a given set of circumstances, and this did not always make him an easy person to skipper.

John was rightly held in high regard by opposing batsmen throughout his long and successful Test career. This, somewhat ironically for me, started at Lord's in 1965 in the Second Test against New Zealand. It was my last appearance for England, but I did not have the opportunity of sharing the new ball with John, who, for the first and last time, was chosen as third seamer. Fred Rumsey was my new-ball partner. Over the ensuing years, it was to be John's misfortune that he seldom had a quality fast bowler to help him at the other end.

All bowlers like batting, but I always felt that John would ideally have preferred to be a high-class batsman. There were certainly times when he did not enjoy bowling, which is rare for a great bowler. Most of them want to bowl too much, and I know I was never really happy in the field unless I was on, or about to come on. Even on those occasions when the ball was turning and

Johnny Wardle and Bob Appleyard were doing the damage – and I knew perfectly well I should not bowl, and would not bowl – I still wanted to, because my job was to take wickets and you can only do that when you're bowling. The only other great bowler who quite often did not want to bowl – and this had nothing to do with a plumb pitch or batsmen in form – was Keith Miller.

The following story from Peter Parfitt perfectly illustrates John's attitude. Middlesex were playing Sussex on a typical Hove wicket that gave the seamers more than a little encouragement. At tea Peter, with a little luck, the odd edge and a life, found himself unbeaten with 80 to his credit, and he thought that if he could see off the threat of John Snow after the interval, there was more than a good chance of his notching up three figures. To his surprise he noticed that John was wearing 'crepes' and asked him why. Much to Peter's delight, John told him that he wouldn't be bowling again that day as he'd done enough already! Perhaps John enjoyed too much liberty at Sussex. He certainly would never have been allowed to get away with that if he'd played for Yorkshire. – F.S.T.

Bob Willis

Although I had seen Bob Willis in action for Surrey, for whom he was a promising, lively, but ungainly bowler, the first time he impressed me was at Sydney in the final Test of the 1970-71 series when England under Ray Illingworth regained the Ashes. Bob, who at twenty-one had been flown out as a replacement for the injured Alan Ward, captured four wickets, including clean-bowling both Chappells in the first innings when they were well set. He also brought off one fine catch and displayed considerable tenacity as a tailender. The combination of his height and his determination, allied to considerable pace and a certain bloody-mindedness which can be such an asset to a fast bowler, suggested that he might possibly develop into something more than that long line of England quickies, among them Alan Ward, John Price, Fred Rumsey, Jeff Jones, David Brown and Len Coldwell, who achieved a certain success without ever consistently returning the figures one expects from an international pace bowler.

Injuries and a row with Surrey that led to his moving to Warwickshire interrupted Bob's international career, but he was chosen to tour Australia in 1974-75, when England were routed by Lillee and Thomson. He bowled fast and well as the spearhead in the first three Tests to capture 15 wickets, but, despite careful nursing, knee injuries reduced his effectiveness thereafter. He had to settle for a wicket apiece in the Fourth and Fifth Tests and was unable to play in the last, or to tour New Zealand.

It was then felt, with some justification, that Bob's international career was over, but he came back at Leeds in 1976 to claim eight wickets in the Fourth Test against the very powerful West Indian side. However, the West Indian batsmen dissected him with relish at The Oval, as they did most of the England bowlers, and once again the critics wrote him off. Again, however, they were wrong, as indeed they were to be proved wrong on several subsequent occasions. That winter, in India, he was the spearhead of England's attack, taking 20 wickets in the Tests, and ever since he has been an almost permanent figure in the England side. In 1979-80, on his fourth tour of Australia, he took only three wickets in the three (all lost) Tests, but 'Big Bob' was to have ample revenge in 1981 at

Headingley, where, with Australia needing 130 to win, he picked up eight wickets in their second innings to bring about a sensational victory for the home team. As a result of that, Bob retained his place, which he had seemed certain to lose, toured India as Fletcher's vice-captain, and was appointed skipper of England the following summer.

Bob comes into the 'charge up and thump it down with heart and life' category of fast bowlers, whose success stems essentially from pace and bounce. There is nothing subtle about his bowling, while his ultra-long run-up and rather full-chested action are certainly not beautiful. But he is effective, as many others of his type have been in the past and will be in the future.

What does surprise, though, is his vast haul of Test wickets and the fact that he has lasted so long. Neither would have happened in any earlier era, when there was less Test cricket than there has been in the last ten to fifteen years. It must also be said that some of the opposition, especially during the World Series Cricket years, was second-class, while the batting line-up of the 1981 Australians was insipid. Another factor to Bob's advantage is that, although lacking the assistance of another quality pace bowler for most of his international career, he has been lucky in that, even when he was finding wickets hard to obtain, he had no serious rival as England's number one spearhead. His rivals, so-called, either lacked Bob's pace and bounce or were well below international standard – and this despite the fact that Bob turned thirty in 1979.

While there are many more Test matches, and therefore the opportunity to take many international wickets, Bob has had to bowl comparatively few overs for Warwickshire. In a decade of Championship cricket with them he has taken less than 300 wickets and bowled less than 2,500 overs. If, with his long run and exhausting style of bowling, he had to send down annually over 1,000 overs per summer, which used to about par for the course, he would have been lucky to retain his international place for so long, because some of his pace and bounce, on which he depends so much, would inevitably have departed.

In 1981 Bob bowled 252 overs for England against Australia in six Tests and took 29 wickets. For Warwickshire, in County Championship matches, he bowled 138 overs and took a mere 13 wickets, while in all first-class matches he sent down 391 overs and captured 42 wickets. It is interesting to compare these figures with those of Fred Trueman in 1961. Fred played in four Tests

Bob Willis, whose right foot points down the pitch,
as will his left foot when he releases the ball,
has an open action with little rock-back.

against the Australians, bowled 164 overs and took 20 wickets. In Championship matches for Yorkshire he sent down 754 overs and took 109 wickets, while in all first-class matches his figures were 1,180.1–302–3,000–155 (average 19.35). Let us take another year at random, 1963, when Fred was nearing the end of his international career. He played in five Tests against West Indies, bowled 236 overs and took 34 wickets. In County Championship matches he captured 76 wickets in 472 overs (average 12.84), and though he bowled only 844 overs in all first-class matches that summer he finished at the top of the national averages with 129 wickets. The considerable difference between the number of overs Fred had to bowl compared with Bob's figures shows that fast bowling is not so demanding over a period of time as it used to be.

It is also intriguing to note that when, at Colchester on 21 August, 1982, Essex scored 502 against Warwickshire, Bob Willis, England's main strike bowler and captain of Warwickshire, sent down only 12 overs and did not bowl at all at McEwan, who plundered a spectacular 128 in 140 minutes. It is inconceivable that Fred would have bowled a mere 12 overs if the opposition were rattling up 500-plus against Yorkshire – especially if a second-line bowler like Kallicharran sent down 46!

A final consideration is the revised lbw law, which forces batsmen to play at balls that pitch well wide of the off stump for fear of being adjudged leg-before, offering no stroke, to a delivery which comes back sharply. This has helped all seam bowlers, but it has been especially beneficial to a pace bowler like Bob who slants the ball in naturally from the angle of his delivery. To hit the middle stump with a straight, good-length ball, he needs to pitch well outside the off stump. The outcome of the revised law is that batsmen are now playing at many balls which in another era they would have ignored.

Bob's long international career has also enabled him to acquire the greatest honour the game has to offer in this country, the England captaincy; this despite the fact that fast bowlers are not ideally suited to the job. Nor could it be said that he is a master tactitian or a natural leader, and so it was not entirely unpredictable that England would lose the Ashes in Australia in 1982-83; or fail to make the finals of the one-day series. In Bob's defence, it should be said that he was given a weak side, but he must take some of the responsibility for the failure of most of his players to perform to their full potential.

On the other hand, it could be said that the captaincy represented a just reward for the numerous times he had acted as
vice-captain, a rather thankless role which he undertook
enthusiastically and successfully. Furthermore, he possesses a
sense of authority, is not a 'yes-man', has his own decided views,
and has the respect of the players. But more to the point, there
were very few alternatives once the new Chairman of Selectors,
Peter May, decided to ditch Keith Fletcher; and he was fortunate
to take over his command against India who, in England, are
rarely formidable. It also helps to be a winning captain, and when
Bob was unable to play in the Second Test against Pakistan,
through injury, the Selectors lumbered his temporary replacement,
David Gower, with an attack which could be described as medium,
mundane and lower-middle-class. Although David could change
his bowlers, it made no real difference because he could not change
his bowling and Pakistan's batsmen were able to compile a decisive
first-innings total. However, when Bob took over again for the
Third Test at Headingley, England won the series with his extra
pace playing a considerable part.

In one respect Bob is a throw-back to a less demonstrative age.
When he is bowling he disappears into a world of his own and,
unless he is reminded by his vice-captain, or a colleague, he is
liable to forget to make necessary adjustments to the field. He is, in
fact, a rather more complex character than is generally imagined.
His emotions are carefully masked, his face usually as expression-
less as his rather flat accent, but like so many big men he is sensitive
to criticism, which he sometimes tries to hide with verbal aggression,
and like most quick bowlers he possesses an intolerant streak. He
thrives on plenty of encouragement when the going is hard, the
wickets are not falling and he is thundering up with his arms and
legs working like pistons on a steam locomotive. This was where
Mike Brearley was so good. – T.E.B.

When I first saw Bob Willis bowl I could not believe it, and after
watching him carefully for some time I said that he couldn't last.
His run-up to the wicket was very long, and rather ungainly as he
had to pump his arms and legs to arrive with sufficient momentum.
Although when he reached his actual delivery stride he used his full
height of six feet six, he was so chest-on and awkward that I was
convinced he would always be breaking down throughout his
career – if he ever had one.

I could not have been more wrong, as he is now one of England's leading wicket-takers with more than 200 victims to his credit. His run-up is still very, very long, but he is one of those bowlers who does need such an approach because it takes him such a long time to move into top gear. Just to give some idea of the length of Bob's run-up: a former colleague came up to me while I was watching Bob in action and said, 'Do you know, Fred, I don't go as far as that on my holidays'.

Bob has already had two, or three, operations on his knee, and has pulled, torn and damaged various other portions of his anatomy, which will surprise nobody who has seen him in action. What he will be like later on in life is what worries me about Bob. But for guts, and for determination to keep on bowling, I do not think anybody has bettered his efforts and achievements. He is full of enthusiasm and strains to bowl hard, fast and take a wicket with every ball. He often amazes me at the amount of bounce he gets on very slow pitches and this is probably his greatest asset. Furthermore, in the last few years Bob Willis has done a great deal for England with his whole-hearted fast bowling without any real pace at the other end. His partners have been fast-medium bowlers like Chris Old, Mike Hendrick, John Lever or Ian Botham, and he has never had the benefit of a genuine, class speed merchant as his new-ball partner. – F.S.T.

Ian Botham

A conversation at The Oval, *1981*

Ian Botham is a true international-class all-rounder, because he is worth his place in the England team both for his batting and his bowling. On top of that, he's also a brilliant all-purpose fielder. He is certainly the most spectacular and successful all-rounder in Test cricket England has produced this century, and you and I have just seen him capture his 200th Test wicket faster than any Englishman. What do you make of it?

It's a difficult question to answer, because Ian is an inconsistent bowler in some respects, despite his great record in Test matches and his very high striking-rate. On the other hand, he does have the ability to produce the unplayable ball more often than most, and this has been the hallmark of all world-class bowlers throughout the ages.

.E.B. It seems to me that there are two reasons why Ian has taken so many wickets. Firstly, he is essentially an attacking bowler whose principal aim is to dismiss opposing batsmen, not to contain them. This is a rare attribute in an age of limited-overs cricket when containment is often the main objective. Secondly, he bowls a full length because he appreciates the value of the swinging half-volley, especially in Test matches. He deliberately invites batsmen to drive him through the covers as three boundaries are a cheap price to pay for a possible catch in the slips off the outside edge.

F.S.T. You're so right about the swinging half-volley, particularly the out-swinger which goes late. I reckon it's the most effective ball I bowled. Ian bowls for wickets, not maidens, and batsmen are more likely to try to take liberties with someone of his pace than with someone quicker.

.E.B. It's noticeable that he is relatively more effective in Test cricket than in one-day games.

F.S.T. He certainly would not be my choice to tie up one end. For that job I'd much rather have somebody like Mike Hendrick, who is so

93

Ian Botham in full follow-through, exuding power and fire.

difficult to score off because he bowls just short of a full length. Ian's attacking approach helps to explain why he has taken five or more wickets in a Test match on no fewer than 17 occasions, whereas Mike has never done it once.

Another reason why Ian is such a prolific wicket-taker is his fine physique. This, combined with an economical run-up, means that he operates for very long spells, and the more overs one bowls the greater the chance of capturing wickets.

E.B. How I wish that vast army of English seamers would copy Ian, instead of employing very long run-ups which do nothing but waste time and energy. He, of course, is different from the average England seamer in that he relies so much more on movement through the air. How would you classify him?

S.T. I agree that Ian is more of a swerve, or swing, bowler than the seamer, who depends on movement after the ball has pitched. What is strange is that his natural movement is away from the bat, despite a high but comparatively open body action.

E.B. In his pursuit of wickets, Ian is always prepared to experiment; using the width of the crease to alter the angle, changing his pace, and following up the out-swinger with a good in-swinger.

S.T. I have always admired bowlers who try to do something different, and though his slower ball is sometimes put away, it does bring him the odd wicket, which is far more important.

E.B. There are times when it seems to me that, for someone of his pace, Ian does overdo the bouncer. But of course he can point to the large number of victims he has secured with it, especially on good pitches when wickets are hard to get. It's probably true to say that he has been assisted by the number of batsmen trying to hook without the necessary ability, but then again he has sensibly exploited this basic weakness. In addition, a bouncer from a fast-medium bowler tends to come as more of a surprise than one from a fast bowler, and there can be no doubt that it has proved to be a profitable weapon in his armoury.

S.T. Because he is such a fine batsman and powerful hooker himself, Ian does not mind whom he lets have the bouncer, which often disconcerts opposing fast bowlers. Ian also has enormous belief in his own ability. Whenever he has the ball he believes he can get the batsman out.

T.E.B.   This self-confidence is a great asset, and in this respect he's rather as you used to be, Fred. Because of his pace he does tend to swing both his outer and his inner fairly early, but in the right conditions he does move them a great deal. In addition to which he makes the odd one come back sharply off the pitch.

F.S.T.   Ian has obviously found the new lbw rule a considerable help, as the batsmen now have to play at out-swingers, which previously they would have left well alone. Consequently, Ian can afford to attack middle and off, whereas I had to try to make my outer go from middle and leg, which is more difficult.

The conversation was continued on the Sydney Cricket Ground in January 1983, after Australia had regained the Ashes rather more easily than a final scoreline of two Tests to one might suggest. Fred had covered the whole series for Australian television and BBC radio and was joined by Trevor, who had gone out for the Fifth Test.

T.E.B.   The thing that has fascinated me most about this Test has been how little England appear to have learnt tactically, despite the fact that this was the fifth encounter. True, they've realised that Wessels is suspect against seam around his leg stump, but this cannot have been too difficult to work out. Any left-hander whose initial movement by his left leg is back to the on side must automatically tend to become tucked up on his leg stump. On the other hand, nobody seemed to appreciate that a deep cover would have prevented a number of boundaries from Wessels, who is a splendid cutter, especially when the bowling is inclined to be short outside off stump. Similarly, for Border, who drives very straight, mid-off and mid-on cannot afford to stand wide.

I also noted that Miller, at first slip, stood both fine and deep so that he appeared to have a very limited catching area. He was covered by the acrobatic Taylor on one side and Botham, who positions himself very close to the stumps at second slip, on the

Ian Botham in Australia in 1982-83, when he was unable to move his
outswinger as he had done in the past. This was probably because he
was not releasing the ball at exactly the right moment.

other. Greg Chappell, who brought off a couple of outstanding first-slip catches, certainly stationed himself much wider.

F.S.T. It's interesting that you should bring up that point. Miller has been at first slip for the England seamers, who have done most of the bowling, for the whole of the tour and has had to make only one catch. That was a rebound off Tavaré!

I have been unable to make any sense of Bob Willis's tactics on a number of occasions. There was the insertion at Adelaide, of all places, and the failure to pressurise the last pair at Melbourne, which allowed them to put on 70, gave Border the chance to play himself back into form, and almost cost us the match. Many times there appeared to be several captains on the field directing operations.

T.E.B. What rather puzzled me at Sydney was our two main strike bowlers, who between them have taken over 500 Test wickets. Willis did relatively little bowling, and Botham looked no more than an adequate third or fourth seamer. How has Ian bowled in this series?

F.S.T. He hasn't been getting his left shoulder round, with the result that he has been opening up too early and has become too chest-on. His dangerous out-swinger, which brought him so many of his wickets, seems to have gone. A lot of his deliveries from the edge of the crease are going straight on, while his in-swinger is starting too early. Often he was 'pushing' it so that it went all the way from the time it left his hand. I'm not certain, but this could be the outcome of a back injury which occurred a year or so ago. What I do know, though, is that he appears to be too heavy for an international opening bowler.

T.E.B. In the Sydney Test, when conditions in Australia's first innings were ideal for moving the ball in the air, Ian did not look like an international-class swing bowler. At his best, I would have expected him to gobble up at least six wickets for very few runs. His away-swinger would have been regularly beating the bat or finding the outside edge, but instead, as you said, he relied mainly on the in-swinger.

Although it is not always realised, perfect timing is just as important in bowling as it is in batting; in fact rather more so. It seemed to me that Ian had lost his timing, with the result that he was releasing the ball a shade too late. Furthermore, he was not rocking back in his action as much as he once did. The outcome was that he was not able to employ some of his most important skills. Firstly, he was having difficulty in bowling his 'outer' and 'nip-backer', and secondly his bouncer, which has brought him many victims over the years, had lost its venom. Indeed, on occasions it sat up and positively smiled at the batsman. It was noticeable that when the ball did pass the bat, it was not hitting Bob Taylor's gloves with a real thwack. Although he was never a fast bowler, in previous Tests against Australia Ian had made their batsmen hurry their shots, even on the slower English pitches. However, I did find it revealing that when, after a long spell, Ian used an abbreviated run-up, his first two deliveries left the bat, because from a short approach his timing returned.

S.T.   Throughout this tour Ian's bowling has lacked its former snap. What worries me is that we could have seen the end of Ian as a high-quality opening bowler, because I must admit that during this series he has not looked the part. His 18 wickets have cost 40 runs apiece.

E.B.   I believe, and certainly hope, that Ian will regain his old form and rhythm, but it will require much hard work on his part and I fear that some of his original incentive may have gone. On the other hand, Ian must want to reclaim his unofficial title of best all-rounder in the world from Imran Khan.

S.T.   I hope you're right, because England cannot afford to be without Botham, the bowler. But it's a pity that there is no other all-rounder to challenge for his place. This is one of the weaknesses of our cricket at the present time – the lack of players who are reasonable alternatives for our established Test men when they are out of form or in the middle of a bad patch.

E.B.   Although Ian did not make as many runs as had been expected in Australia, he was still worth his place as a batsman. It seemed to me that he was trying to recreate the magic of those incredible innings at Headingley and Old Trafford – two of the finest exhibitions of calculated, brutal hitting I have ever witnessed – because he desperately wanted to show the hostile Australian crowd exactly what he could do with the bat. By his own, almost impossibly high standard. it was not a good tour, but he still demonstrated his immense value to the team by capturing the most wickets and taking more catches than anybody else, including Bob Taylor behind the stumps!

Australian Pace Bowlers

Australian Pace Bowlers

Trevor Bailey

One of the biggest mistakes in the game is to underestimate the ability and the penetration of Australian pace bowlers, because they have the knack of proving to be, especially in England, far more formidable than expected. The following are just a few examples of how they will suddenly emerge from comparative obscurity and make a major impact at international level.

The selection of Terry Alderman as a member of Kim Hughes's 1981 touring party came as a considerable surprise to many, and a number would have preferred to see Jeff Thomson as Lillee's opening partner. Alderman had never played in a Test and was not exceptionally fast, but nevertheless this well-built, fast-medium seamer proceeded to capture 42 wickets in the six Tests. In normal circumstances, this would have been more than sufficient to win the Ashes for Australia.

The Australian team which toured England in 1972 under Ian Chappell was reckoned by the experts to have little chance. After all, Australia had surrendered the Ashes to Ray Illingworth and company in 1970-71 and had been annihilated by South Africa the season before that. Instead, the series was shared 2-2, and one of the main reasons for the Australians' success was the unexpected support which the almost unknown Bob Massie provided for their spearhead, Dennis Lillee. Massie's Test début at Lord's was the most sensational ever. He took eight for 84 and eight for 53 with what was surely the most devastating exhibition of swerve bowling seen in England.

More than a decade earlier, in 1961, Graham McKenzie made his first England tour as a promising twenty-year-old. In his first Test – also, like Massie's, at Lord's – he captured five wickets for 37 in the second innings, which not only helped Australia to victory but also heralded the arrival of another outstanding international fast bowler.

Although Australian novice fast bowlers have done remarkably well in England, where conditions will assist them once they realise the need to bowl an English length and pitch the ball up a little further than in their own country, there have also been instances of their causing havoc at home.

102

The most sensational was the arrival of Jeff Thomson, who provided a deadly barrage which flattened, sometimes literally, the hopes of Mike Denness's touring team in 1974-75. But in some respects, even more remarkable was the appearance of Rodney Hogg against England in 1978-79 at the somewhat advanced age, for a 'quickie', of twenty-seven. Hogg had played only two not very successful seasons of first-class cricket, and it is unlikely that he would have caught the eye of his Selectors had Australia not been reduced to fielding what was basically a second XI because virtually all their best players were contracted to World Series Cricket. However, Hogg made the best possible use of his opportunity, taking 41 wickets in the six Tests to break Arthur Mailey's record for an Australian against England of 36, taken in five Tests back in 1920-21. What makes Hogg's performance, which was obtained by bowling fast and straight in short, sharp spells, even more remarkable was that England were triumphant in five of the six Tests, his 41 wickets only cost just over 12 runs apiece, and his support was limited.

In 1982-83, the Australians were expected to build their attack around Lillee and Alderman, who had proved so effective in England in 1981, with the main support coming from Geoff Lawson, who had promised much on the same tour until he broke down. However, by the end of the First Test they had lost both Alderman, injured as a result of an injudicious tackle on a spectator, and Lillee, who had to have a knee operation. Furthermore, Rackemann, brought in for the Second Test, broke down in that match. Yet in spite of these considerable set-backs, the sustained thrust of Lawson, combined with the speed of Thomson and Hogg – both still fast enough to upset a rather insipid England batting line-up – proved sufficient for Australia to win the Third Test by eight wickets and go on to take the series.

Australian cricket in the thirties was dominated largely by the genius of Sir Donald Bradman and the spin bowling of Clarrie Grimmett and Bill O'Reilly. Although there were some good fast bowlers, including 'Tim' Wall and Ernie McCormick, the majority of their Test victories stemmed from a combination of Bradman's bat and their wrist-spinners. The surprising feature about both Wall and McCormick was that, unlike their post-war counterparts, neither was particularly impressive nor effective in England, though the latter caused a sensation by being no-balled no less than 35 times in the 1938 Australians' opening match at Worcester.

Max Walker: 'He bowled off the wrong foot, his feet criss-crossed awkwardly in his pre-delivery stride – hence the nickname of "Tanglefoot" – and he was very open-chested.' Yet here was an artist.

Geoff Lawson in the early 1980s became the latest in the line
of truly fast bowlers Australia has produced.
His pace and hostility, good control, and his variation of line
and movement proved too much for England's batsmen in 1982 83.

In sharp contrast, the outstanding feature of Australian cricket since 1946 has been the pace and penetration of their fast bowlers. Even though their 1948 side possessed probably the most formidable batting line-up Australia has produced, it was Lindwall, Miller and Johnston who really destroyed England. Since then, Australian teams, whether outstanding, highly competent or mundane, have all contained at least two excellent seamers, a well-above-average wicket-keeper and some good batsmen.

The big Australian weakness in England since the war has been their slow bowlers, who have been largely ineffectual. Their finger-spinners, whether left-armers or off-break bowlers, have seldom been as good as their English counterparts in county teams; indeed, many have been decidedly inferior. One gained the impression that some of their slow left-armers were picked on the assumption that they ought to do well in England, rather than on ability. The same thinking applied to a number of wrist-spinners England have sent to Australia as a result of the theory that they were essential and the equally strange theory that it was pointless taking an off-spinner – though taking three, as in 1982-83, does seem to be an excessive swing in the other direction.

The lack of match-winning Australian spinners in England is certainly borne out by the figures. Of the 786 English batsmen who have been dismissed in Tests by their bowlers since 1948, no fewer than 628 have fallen to seamers, while the total haul for spinners, who arguably include Ernie Toshack, is a mere 158, representing rather less than one wicket per innings.

Why has Australia produced so many top-quality opening bowlers in the last forty years; more indeed than any other country including England? One important reason is that, because in general their pitches are less sympathetic, they have to work much harder for success than their English counterparts. At an early age they realise that it is not enough to bowl well within themselves, maintain a reasonable line and length, and rely on the wicket to do the rest – which, of course, is exactly what it is possible to do on so many English 'green tops'. Line and length remain important, but these two classic ingredients are not enough on their own and the Australian seamer has to look further if he is to have any chance of reaching the top.

There are three alternatives open to him. Firstly, he can aim to become a real quickie, assuming he has been given the ability to bowl at great speed. (It is impossible to make a fast bowler, unless he has been given the ability to propel a cricket ball with exceptional speed.) In England, on our slower pitches, the accurate seamer is often more effective and economical than the real quickie, who initially is likely to be somewhat erratic. Consequently there is not quite the same incentive, as there is in Australia, to strive to become the fastest bowler around. Jeff Thomson, whose main weapon has always been speed, provides the perfect example of what it can achieve.

In general it would also be true to say that Australians enjoy bowling, and indeed playing cricket, rather more than an England county cricketer who is often playing seven days a week. It is, after all, asking a great deal of someone to bowl flat out day in, day out. There is an obvious temptation these days for him to cruise for some of the time so that he has that extra for the big occasion.

Secondly, the Australian seamer, once he realises that he can never be another Thomson or Lawson, can think in terms of becoming a fast-medium bowler, quick enough to make a batsman hurry his shots and to bowl a respectable bouncer but seldom quick enough to escape punishment when he bowls a bad ball. He, therefore, must master line and length, but alone that will not be sufficient. He has to learn to achieve some movement off the pitch by cutting his fingers down the side of the ball, to use the crease in order to change the angle of delivery, and to vary his pace.

Australian cricket has always abounded with high-quality fast-medium seamers, some of whom never achieved the success at the highest level that their ability warranted. I always felt that Geoff Noblet fell into that category. He was one of the most accomplished seamers I encountered in Australia, despite (or perhaps because of) having to play all his home matches at Adelaide, the best batting wicket in the country. He never toured England, where he would have enjoyed himself, and was chosen for only three Tests. He possessed all the best qualities of an Australian fast-medium bowler: control, change of pace, ability to move the ball in the air and off the wicket, a slower delivery that was hard to pick, and a distinctly useful bouncer. He had a high, whippy action, which might perhaps have been a little too whippy for English umpires, but he was certainly no worse than many others and he was never no-balled for throwing in Australia or South Africa, where he toured in 1949-50.

I first saw Max Walker bowling in Sabina Park against West Indies in 1972-73, and my initial reaction was to wonder why he had been selected for the tour. He bowled off the wrong foot, his feet criss-crossed awkwardly in his pre-delivery stride – hence the nickname of 'Tanglefoot' – he was very open-chested and his pace was unexceptional. However, I soon realised my mistake. Here was an artist who bowled big late in-swingers, gave nothing away, used his considerable height to good effect and was able to keep going for long spells. On that occasion his figures were a very impressive 39–10–114–6, which, as West Indies put together a total of 428, illustrated his value as a dual-purpose bowler. With Lillee injured and Massie out of touch in this series, Max became the main Australian strike bowler, and his 26 wickets on good batting pitches against a powerful batting side were one of the main reasons why Ian Chappell's team, rather surprisingly, won the rubber.

In 1974-75, when Lillee and Thomson formed his country's spearhead, Walker took over as third seamer and still picked up 23 wickets in the six Tests against England. As one would expect from a basic in-swing bowler with an open-chested action, he acquired a genuine leg-cutter, as distinct from the ball which happens to hit the seam and behaves in the same fashion. In England Max would have taken more wickets if he had been prepared to bowl a slightly fuller length and had occasionally employed a couple of leg-slips. Time and time again he would beat the bat with the leg-cutter pitched outside the line of the off stump, whereas this would have been a wicket-taker had it been pitched between wicket and wicket.

Alan Connolly, having started off as a fast bowler without ever possessing quite enough speed, reduced his run-up and became an outstanding fast-medium bowler who relied on a mixture of cut, swerve and change of pace for his considerable success. Although he took more wickets for Victoria that any other bowler, his haul would have been greater but for the back trouble which plagued him throughout his career. However, I do not think anybody epitomises the Australian fast-medium seamer better than Terry Alderman in that summer of 1981 – tall, well-built and accurate, he bowled with consistent hostility and exceptional stamina.

The third alternative for the ambitious Australian quickie lacking those extra yards of pace is to learn to swing the ball in the air, although there will be times when he will find it difficult to swerve it, and so will be a seam rather than a swing bowler. Two Australian new-ball bowlers whom I always think of primarily as purveyors of swerve, because it was this ability which constituted their biggest threat, are Hawke and Massie. (Alan Davidson also had this ability as part of his armoury.) Bob Massie, who started so well, suddenly lost his ability to swing the ball and in a very short time was unable to command a place in his state side. Neil Hawke was essentially an arm bowler with an ugly, rather crab-like, open action, but he was none the less an extremely effective opening bowler who dipped the ball very late in to the right-hander. A thoughtful, intelligent bowler who realised that it paid to bowl a full length if the ball was swinging, he later developed an effective out-swinger and used cut and change of pace as additional weapons.

Lindwall and Miller

All bowlers are more formidable when they can hunt in pairs, but this applies especially to fast bowlers because it ensures that there is no escape to the other end for the wretched, sometimes frightened, batsmen. Gregory and McDonald, Larwood and Voce, Lindwall and Miller, Trueman and Statham, Lillee and Thomson: the legendary partnerships come immediately to mind. And of all these outstanding pace combinations, none was more talented and menacing than that of Ray Lindwall and Keith Miller, for in addition to being genuinely fast they were highly talented operators who had many other weapons in their armoury.

They were also completely dissimilar in style, method, approach and character. Ray, with his flowing run-up, toe-drag and low arm action, was a beautiful bowling machine; Keith, with his short gallop to the stumps and his high rocking action, was entirely unpredictable and sometimes unplayable. Invariably exciting, his bowling reminded me of a cavalier cavalry charge, full of fire, dash, flair and courage, but a little lacking in discipline.

Ray Lindwall was the complete fast bowler, an artist. In addition to sheer speed, he had an approach and body action that were a joy to behold, stamina, a splendid physique with very powerful shoulders, swerve, change of pace, and fine bouncer – he was the only bowler to injure me seriously when I successfully dropped his bouncer dead at my feet in a Sydney Test, but made the mistake of using my thumb instead of the bat. Most important of all, he possessed greater control than any other really quick bowler I have encountered. As a result, like Trueman and Lillee after him, he was able to go on taking Test wickets long after he had lost some of his original pace through the air.

How quick was Lindwall in his early days? Denis Compton and Bill Edrich believe that he was at his fastest during MCC's 1946-47 tour to Australia, though to what extent this was due to the fact that they were encountering real speed for the first time since before the war, and because fast bowlers are always faster in Australia than in England, it is difficult to say. There is, however, no doubt that Ray's quicker ball during his first tour to England in 1948 was as fast as anything I have seen since.

From a spectator's point of view, the run-up of a genuine fast bowler is one of the game's most exhilarating sights. It should start slowly and gradually work up to a peak the moment before he moves into the delivery stride. The body action should combine power with grace before it gradually fades into a full follow-through. Ray fulfilled all these requirements, and he avoided that frequent modern complaint of an over-long approach which wastes both time and energy. His run-up of just under twenty walking paces never varied. A batsman had no chance of picking his bouncer until the ball had been released, while Ray's ability to slip in the extra-fast yorker at will made him so difficult to play. He also bowled a cleverly camouflaged slow ball, which takes a long time and much practice for a fast bowler, unless he is a thrower, to deliver effectively. The one unusual feature of Ray's action was that his bowling arm was low. This, when combined with his long drag, meant that he achieved less deviation off the seam with the old ball than Miller, who had a high action and therefore a much steeper delivery.

Ray was the first of the great post-war draggers. At that time this method had several advantages, apart from eliminating the jump, which outweighed the disadvantage of losing some height when releasing the ball. The Australian umpires did not mind if a bowler dropped behind and then dragged through the bowling crease, which meant that the dragger could release the ball much closer to the batsman than a bowler with the traditional catapult, or rocking, action. English umpires were less tolerant and insisted that the draggers had to land a foot or so behind the bowling crease; but Ray's control was so good that he had no difficulty adapting.

Ray Lindwall swung the ball much more than any other genuinely fast bowler I have seen, which is why he was such a deadly exponent with the new ball. A common failing in all forms of cricket is to waste the new ball by not bowling at the stumps, although this is less of a crime today because of the current lbw Law, and controlling the amount of swerve is a major problem for a swing bowler. If he aims at the off stump, the ball is likely to do too much; but if, when he switches to the leg stump, it fails to move, the batsman is able to help himself to easy runs on the leg side. Ray, however, possessed that rare skill of being able to start his away-swing from *outside* the leg stump, with the result that he would sometimes have a batsman caught in the gully off the

Ray Lindwall, about to start his toe-drag and looking over his
straight left arm. Compare the position of his right foot with
Fred Trueman's on page 70.

Ray Lindwall nears the end of his drag. This picture was taken in England, where the umpires had forced him to commence his drag well behind the bowling crease. In Australia, at the same stage, his left foot would already have been in front of the batting crease.

outside edge as he attempted to push the ball through the on side.

It is doubtful if anything, even slow over-rates, has done more over the years to reduce the game as a spectacle than the amendment of the lbw Law in the mid-thirties. In essence it meant that it was no longer necessary to pitch within wicket and wicket to obtain an lbw decision, and this inevitably led to a great increase of in-swing, in-slant bowling and on-side play. In turn, there was a reduction in the number of bowlers who made the ball leave the bat and of off-side strokes by batsmen. Not surprisingly, there have been numerous campaigns for a return to the old lbw Law, with some compensating factor for the bowler, such as a smaller ball or a larger wicket. In the fifties, Lindwall was asked to demonstrate in the nets at Lord's what he could do with a smaller ball, and, despite swinging the ball even more than usual, he gave a fascinating display of his control by repeatedly hitting whichever stump he nominated.

My first encounter with Keith Miller as a bowler was during a wartime game at Hove. I was playing for the Royal Navy. Keith, who was in the RAF, had already acquired a considerable reputation as a dashing strokemaker, but he was unknown as a bowler, and so I thought little of it when, in the middle of my enjoyment of batting against some distinctly friendly bowling, the captain of the opposition tossed the ball to him. He ambled up from a few paces and I am still not sure who was more surprised – the 'keeper, who was standing up, or myself. The first ball, the fastest I have ever received from a fifth-change bowler, sped through for four byes before either of us had moved.

When Keith returned to England in 1948 as a key member of Don Bradman's all-conquering party, he had established himself as Lindwall's new-ball partner. He used an easy, short run-up in conjunction with a graceful, high action which, as he was tall and loose-limbed, enabled him to achieve considerable lift from only just short of a length. Although he did swing the ball at times, he, unlike Lindwall, was more of a seam than a swerve bowler.

Of all the great bowlers Keith derived less pleasure from bowling than any of them. There were times when he simply did not want to bowl and became bored with the idea. I could never fully understand anyone with so much talent not wanting to bowl, but it was probably this characteristic, combined with a volatile temperament, which made his bowling so unpredictable and often devastating. It all came so naturally to Keith that he could drop the ball during his run-up, swoop down, pick it up in one casual movement and carry on bowling as if nothing untoward had happened. He might suddenly unleash a barrage of bouncers, if he happened to feel that way, but he was just as likely to introduce a googly into the proceedings. The one certainty was that the game was never dull when Keith was bowling.

From a career in which he captured 170 wickets in 55 Tests, the majority of which were played on good batting pitches against powerful batting line-ups, it is not really possible to select his finest spell of bowling, though many might select then ten wickets he took at Lord's in 1956, or the time he routed Wally Hammond's team at Brisbane in 1946-47 by taking seven for 60 with Hutton, Washbrook, Edrich and Compton as his first four victims. Myself, I treasure most his opening spell in our second innings of the Adelaide Test of 1954-55. We required just 94 to win the match and so retain the Ashes; the pitch was slow and easy; Lindwall was not playing. It all looked so very simple, but we underestimated what Keith could achieve, even in conditions that favoured the batsmen. He tore into us and in a spell of very high-class bowling removed Hutton, Edrich and Cowdrey in the course of twenty balls. We were eventually thankful to limp home. – T.E.B.

 In the art of fast bowling Ray Lindwall has no peer. To me he was the greatest of them all. The statement of the late Wally Grout really sums it all up. 'He's a fast bowler of the highest class with the movement and the accuracy more associated with an outstanding medium-pace bowler.'

Although Ray did not possess the high classical action of the copybook pace bowler – his was low with more than a suggestion of a sling – he made the ball leave the right-hand batsman, the sure hallmark of most of the greats. The late out-swinger combined with the one that came sharply back off the seam were his stock deliveries, but later in his career he did learn to bowl a very good, effective in-swinger. Yet if it had not been for circumstances, and a twist of fate, it is doubtful whether Ray would have bothered to acquire this new skill, even though it did add a fresh dimension – rather in the same way as a googly does for a leg-spinner. Ironically, Ray's in-swinger was born out of necessity in a lower grade of cricket when he went to play in the Lancashire League. There he found that not only was he regularly beating the outside edge with pace and swerve, but also there was a tendency for the slips to put down the catch if the batsmen did get an edge, especially early in the match.

It quickly dawned on Ray, who was a most intelligent bowler, that he would pick up more wickets if he relied rather less on his fielders and rather more on hitting the stumps. An in-swinger was the obvious answer, especially as a number of the opposing batsmen were liable to 'leave a gate'. With typical Lindwall resolve and patience, plus plenty of time to practise, Ray went into the nets to master this new technique. It took time, but eventual results proved the effort worthwhile because, unlike so many out-swing bowlers who do this and end up with an inner which goes early and is pushed into the batsman, Ray produced an inner which dipped in fast, late and went a long way. He had added another weapon to his armoury and one which was especially useful against ordinary batsmen who simply were not good enough to touch his out-swinger.

When I was touring Australia with MCC in 1958-59, Ray had moved from his native New South Wales to Queensland, and it was at a reception in Brisbane that I heard one of the speakers say something I have always treasured. 'I was brought up to believe that "Satchmo", the one and only Louis Armstrong, was the king of swing,' he told us, 'but I'm no longer so sure after seeing "Lindy" bowl today!'

Ray had the most rhythmical accelerating run-up I have ever seen. As a result, he was so beautifully balanced when he went into his delivery stride that it was very rare for him to miss out on the co-ordination from which his control stemmed. I have always thought that if Beethoven had loved cricket and seen Lindwall bowl, he would have written another symphony.

In addition to his pace and action, Ray had three other essential attributes. Firstly, he was a fine, natural athlete who moved well and excelled at other sports. Secondly, when he was bowling he had a killer instinct which enabled him to produce that little extra venom when it was most needed. And finally he had the stamina and the heart that enabled him to come back at the end of a long hot day.

I do not believe I shall see the likes of Ray Lindwall again, but I do have the memory of talking to him and playing against him. I hope readers will not think I have enthused too much about him, but how can I overpraise? After all, I have been writing about my one and only fast-bowling idol. Indeed, it was often suggested that

Natural and physical. Keith Miller, having swung right round
in releasing the ball, bursts into his follow-through.

I had modelled my bowling on Ray Lindwall, because there were a number of similarities, but this was not true. I had never seen Ray bowl until I played against him. Mind you, if I had been lucky enough to see him bowling when I was a kid, I am sure I would have said then, as I say now, 'That's the way to bowl fast'.

Keith Miller was, for my money, the man's man of cricket. He will go down in history not only as one of the greatest all-rounders ever, but also as one of the game's outstanding entertainers. It is difficult to think of anything he did not do brilliantly, whether batting, bowling or fielding – but especially bowling. In a single over I have seen him bowl six different deliveries: an out-swinger, an in-swinger, a break-back, a bouncer, a very fast yorker and a leg-break. In addition to the leg-break he could send down a good googly, and I remember him slipping one in first over with the new ball against David Sheppard, now the Bishop of Liverpool. Furthermore he had him out lbw with it – what an end for a prelate!

Keith was a magnificent athlete in every sense. Tall and loose-limbed, he was one of those fast bowlers who could make the ball lift sharply from only just short of a length and hit the batsman. He could literally bowl from anywhere and was just as quick off a few paces as off his measured run. The story was that he never really bothered to mark one out but simply walked back, stopped and said, 'That will do for today'.

I have always thought that Keith was an enigma on a cricket field, because nobody knew what he was going to do with bat, ball or in the field; or how he would react to any situation that might arise during a match. It could be mid-afternoon, the pitch looking easy-paced and nothing much happening. Then Keith would take the ball, there would be a buzz of excitement in the crowd, and everything would change. Suddenly the pitch would seem to come to life, the ball would start moving around, and inside a few overs he might well have changed the course of the game. I have no idea what it took to make him inspired, but it certainly happened.

But for all that Keith was the most carefree, casual cricketer I have encountered at international level (at least that's the impression he gave) he did possess a very sharp cricket brain. He always knew what he was trying to do. This factor, combined with his volatile temperament, speed and high action, helped to make him one of the great fast bowlers; a match-winner who was essentially an attacker, always prepared to sacrifice runs in the pursuit of wickets.

In addition to his bowling, Keith was a magnificent attacking batsman and a slip fielder of the highest class. One of the first occasions I saw him bat was in a Combined Services match when he was put down first ball and went on to make considerably more than 200 in well under a day. My figures were none for 96. I was surprised not only by the power and the range of his attacking strokes, but also by their ease and grace. Thinking of Keith in the slips, I can still picture him at The Oval with his arms folded, his legs crossed and looking towards square-leg as Ray Lindwall went into his delivery stride. A moment later he was lying full length, looking down the wicket with the ball – caught inches off the ground – clasped in his left hand. It was an incredible catch which should never have happened. But because Keith was something special, it had.

Off the field Keith was a great person to know. He was always willing to help and give advice, if you asked him, while he remains a good, distinctly lively companion. One of the great thrills for me was when he flew in from Australia to take part in my 'This is Your Life' television programme. He came on last and there were tears in his eyes because he was not just a marvellous all-rounder but he is also a great human being. I am glad to be one of his friends as well as one of his most devoted admirers. He really could play cricket, that one. – F.S.T.

Bill Johnston

It has always seemed to me that the bowling of Bill Johnston never received the credit it deserved. There is a tendency to think of him as just another very good Australian fast-medium bowler – unless you happen to have batted against him, or have examined his record and noted that he took 160 wickets in only 40 Tests, *mainly as the third seamer!* This meant he seldom had the benefit of the new ball, and it should be remembered that the shine did not last nearly so long in his era. Furthermore, he often did not get on, or at least not for long, when the conditions favoured his type of bowling. Yet he took his 100 wickets in Test cricket in just over four years which, in those days of comparatively few internationals, was faster than anybody else.

One of the reasons why Bill has seldom had sufficient acclaim is that he had to live under the shadow of Lindwall and Miller, the main stars of a very powerful attack. Nor did he look the part as he loped up to the stumps amid a flurry of rather gangling arms and legs which tended to camouflage the efficiency and the intent of a very good, high, basic body action with a controlled follow-through.

Another reason is that he was an essentially jovial person with a voice which was ideal for delivering funny comments and droll homilies – characteristics one hopes to find in a good publican, which he now is, but not normally encountered in a fast bowler. Bill was too lovable, too kind, too amusing and too humorous. One felt he really enjoyed the joke of finishing with a final batting average of 102 in 1953, the result of a totally improbable series of not outs, rather more than the wickets he took.

However, Bill, despite his casualness and easy-going nature, did take his bowling seriously. Had he not, he would never have become a truly great Australian seamer. Although not as quick as Lindwall and Miller, he was a fast rather than a fast-medium bowler; about the same pace as Alan Davidson, who also bowled mainly left-arm over the wicket. Because of his height, his bounce was steeper than Alan's but he did not dip the ball into the right-hand batsman quite as sharply in the air. On the other hand, his movement away from the bat off the seam was probably greater, as might be expected from someone who could bowl

Bill Johnston here combines spin and speed to cut the ball away from the right-hand batsman at about medium pace.

left-arm orthodox spinners at about slow-medium quite efficiently.

I would without doubt rate Bill Johnston as the best left-arm pace bowler, other than Alan Davidson, since the Second World War. – T.E.B.

Although I played against Bill Johnston on one occasion, in the final Test of 1953 at The Oval, I never got to know him as a person; and reading what Trevor has written about him, I realise what I missed. I picture him as the perfect third seamer, tall with a high action and deceptively casual lope to the wicket. But, to be honest, I remember him most for that freak average he acquired as a tail-end batsman. That he was able to leave England with a batting average of 102 was due to the number of stars he acquired, not to his ability as a batsman, and I am sure that he, like the majority of fast bowlers, enjoyed taking the micky out of his fellow-bowlers. – F.S.T.

Alan Davidson

When I first met Alan Davidson, he was rather overshadowed by Ray Lindwall and Keith Miller. An occasional member of the New South Wales side, he was none the less a superlative outfield with a great arm, a useful left-arm seamer and hard-hitting lower-order batsman, and so I was not surprised when he was selected for the 1953 tour to England as one of a trio of highly promising young all-rounders, the others being Richie Benaud and Ron Archer. Although Australia had three great pace bowlers, Lindwall, Miller and Johnston, in their party, Alan still managed to force himself into their Test team, being chosen for all five, and enjoyed a most successful first visit.

This is what I wrote about him after that series: 'He is a genuine all-rounder, hard-hitting left-hand bat, a very lively fast-medium bowler and perhaps the best all-positions fielder in a team of exceptional fieldsmen. In character with most other members of the side, Alan smote the ball with whole-hearted vigour so that silly mid-off was never a habitable position. His bowling was accurate rather than devastating.'

In other words, a new international all-rounder had arrived on the scene, and this is exactly how I regarded him for several years – a fine 'bits and pieces' cricketer at Test level. Never did I imagine that he would become, for a period, the most feared new-ball bowler in the world. In retrospect, I suppose I should have realised what was about to happen during the final Test at Sydney in 1954-55. Plagued by various injuries, Alan had not had a particularly successful season against us; but in the last contest, after we had retained the Ashes, Alan was chosen as the third, rather than fourth, seamer and was given the second new (and shiny) ball.

When the new ball was taken, I had been occupying the crease for quite a while and was happily employing the forward defensive, as was my wont, intermingled with the occasional push, cut and edge. Suddenly, to my surprise, a ball of full length dipped in very late from outside off stump and hit me rather painfully on my left foot. This happened twice more, and only the fact that I was so far forward saved me from being lbw, though I was probably still rather lucky to be given the benefit of the doubt.

It was this ability to swing the ball into the right-handed batsman from over the wicket that transformed Alan from a good Test bowler into a great one. Until then, one simply played him as a normal quick left-armer whose line automatically slanted the ball across the right-hander, but when he began to move the odd ball back into the stumps one was forced to play at deliveries one would normally have left severely alone. This sows doubts in the mind and makes batting much more difficult. Ken Barrington, who was England's most consistent run accumulator in the sixties, and who possessed the best defensive technique, always found Alan a problem with the new ball. He certainly would not have done had Alan not developed that ability to move the ball back, as well as run it away. However, it is not an easy art to acquire and may well take years, as it did Alan, to acquire. But the rewards are high.

Should anybody feel I have over-stressed the difference being able to move the ball back into right-handers makes to a left-arm seam bowler, he should study the record of the Surrey bowler, David Sydenham. For years David was just another typical county seamer of comfortable pace. One rather fancied batting against him because he was unlikely to beat the bat if one played straight. Then, after years of practice in the nets, he perfected the knack of making the ball swing either in or away on the line of the right-hander's stump, and from being just another steady bowler who was never too certain of his place in the county side, he captured over a hundred wickets in 1962 and 1963.

Like those of all the successful Australian pace bowlers, Alan's length and direction were invariably superb and, perhaps because he did not have to play too much cricket, his pace was sharp; nearer fast than fast-medium. He had an unpleasant bouncer, which was made all the more effective because he employed it occasionally and did not telegraph it. His run-up was short, around thirteen paces, and he used an easy, loping approach until he accelerated into his delivery stride. He came down hard on a braced right leg with his right foot pointing towards third man, while his follow-through was a model with his left arm chasing his right across his body until checked by his right hip. – T.E.B.

Alan Davidson was the most accomplished left-arm opening bowler I played against. From a brief, easy, athletic run-up, he went into a beautifully sideways-on action which enabled him to swing the ball into the right-hand batsman from on and outside his off

Bowling left arm over the wicket, Alan Davidson released the ball
off a perfectly braced right leg. The left arm swung naturally
across his body as his right foot swivelled

stump. And in addition to being able to dip the ball, he had two other vital assets. He hit the pitch with the seam and was able to make the ball leave the right-hander off the wicket – the left-armer's equivalent of the right-armer's 'nip-backer' – and secondly he slanted the ball across the right-hander as a result of the angle obtained by any left-arm bowler going over the wicket.

It took 'Davo' a long time to reach the top of his trade, because in his youth Lindwall, Miller and Walker were in the New South Wales side, which meant that he seldom got the chance to bowl on a helpful pitch or with the new ball. Most of his bowling had to be done on plumb wickets, although the accuracy this demanded was to prove an asset in the long term. He was not fast in the Lindwall or Thomson sense, but he did possess a genuine bouncer, made all the more effective because it was used sparingly. Strangely for a fast bowler with a splendid physique, he was a confirmed hypo-chondriac – never completely fit and always suffering from some mysterious ache or pain. His colleagues reckoned that he spent more time on the treatment table than the rest of the touring party.

My friendship with Alan grew not only from cricket and the fact that we took the new ball for our respective countries, but also from our mutual love for Rugby League football. We have spent a great deal of time talking about this marvellous game, often joined by Norman O'Neill, another big enthusiast.

In addition to his bowling, Alan was a world-class all-rounder – a hard-hitting left-hand batsman who had the ability to transform the course of a Test match in a very short time, as he did at Old Trafford in 1961, and a superb fieldsman with a marvellous pair of hands. He was not just a hard hitter but he was also a very long hitter, and therefore it is appropriate that I should tell this Neil Hawke story of the time Davo, for once, was on the receiving end.

Gary Sobers, playing for South Australia against New South Wales at Adelaide, was in devastating form with the bat, and the sight of the New South Wales attack being massacred by Gary in full flow was one of the greatest the game has ever known. Richie Benaud went up to Davo, told him he had had enough of the panto, and gave him the ball. Gary predictably accepted the challenge and almost immediately he hit Alan over long-on to the scoreboard. At Adelaide, that is one big, big hit! – F.S.T.

Graham McKenzie

Graham McKenzie made his début for Australia at Lord's in 1961, just a few days before his twenty-first birthday, and immediately struck up a great partnership with Alan Davidson. I had the satisfaction of bowling him on the Saturday morning and immediately wished him a happy birthday. It certainly turned out to be just that, because he celebrated by taking five for 37 in our second innings in 29 overs and his performance played a major part in his team's victory.

I have always thought of Graham as a rhythm bowler with a short, bounding approach and a classical sideways-on action. When not 'clicking' he was liable to spray the ball around, especially in his early days. But if his timing was right he was sharp and hostile on any wicket, not just those favouring pace bowling.

F.S.T.   There was no doubt about that. Graham had all the basic ingredients of a top-class fast bowler – a positive approach, feet in the right position, a full and powerful body action, a high right arm and the ability to move the ball away. And because he 'hit the deck', he made the ball bounce unpleasantly from only just short of a length. That's how he came to break Geoff Boycott's thumb before the Sydney Test of 1970-71.

Not only was Graham a fine fast bowler, but he looked the part too. He had a truly magnificent physique, which is why he acquired the nickname of 'Garth', and his build, plus his economical run-up, meant that he seldom broke down. Which was just as well for Australia, because when Davidson retired Graham was often used for long spells that would have been too much for most quickies. Indeed, his heavy workload may have led to his Test career ending sooner than it might have done had he not had to bowl quite so much. Fortunately he possessed a big heart to match his fine physique, and he was never one to question his captain. He simply kept on bowling to the best of his ability.

T.E.B.   In his 60 Tests Garth took 246 wickets at 29.78, which made him for a time the leading wicket-taker among Australian pacemen. When

The photograph explains why Graham McKenzie was able to obtain so much pace from his short bounding approach and illustrates his dependence on perfect timing.

his Test days were over, he continued to give outstanding service to Leicestershire for several more years, and one often felt that his country might have dispensed with his services too soon.

The abbreviated run-up demanded by the John Player League, which was introduced to suit the particular needs of Sunday television, had an adverse effect on most fast bowlers because they were unable to generate their normal speed using such a short approach. They became fast-medium rather than fast. Garth, however, was an exception; because his pace was derived mainly from a lithe body action and did not require a long run-up, he seemed almost as quick for Leicestershire on Sundays as he did during the week.

S.T. All Australians hate losing and Garth was no exception. He was often at his best with both ball and bat when the enemy seemed to have won, but he was far removed from most Australian sportsmen in that he was quiet, shy and unassuming; a gentle giant. As Christopher Martin-Jenkins so aptly wrote in his *Who's Who of Test Cricketers*: 'He was a gentleman on and off the field who never abused his strength and speed.'

E.B. Fred implied earlier that Graham greatly missed the presence of Alan Davidson, when Alan retired. But although he found himself without a partner at the other end of the same high quality, he still turned in many fine performances for Australia and made no less than eight overseas tours during his decade at the top. His most unsuccessful was his last, to South Africa in 1969-70, when the Australian Board of Control made the monumental mistake of going there immediately after a gruelling visit to India and he managed only one wicket for 333 runs in three Tests.

To appreciate the stupidity of this decision, it must be remembered that a five-Test tour to India is invariably very demanding, while at that time South Africa had probably the best side in the world. To go straight from the slow pitches of India, where Graham bowled almost 300 overs, to South Africa, who had a fine batting line-up, was madness, and the massacre which followed was entirely predictable.

Not surprisingly, Garth looked stale against Ray Illingworth's team in Australia the following winter and lost his place. However, I believe that if he had been included in the last and deciding match at Sydney, Australia would not have lost the series. Moreover, he would then have been chosen for his fourth tour to England. The pitch on which England batted on the first morning was ideal for pace bowling, but the young Lillee, lacking experience, and Dell, who was not of international standard, failed to exploit it properly.

Lillee and Thomson

Whenever, or wherever, fast bowling is discussed, the name Dennis Lillee is bound to be mentioned, for he unquestionably is one of the all-time great quick bowlers in the game. As far as I am concerned, he is the last of what I would describe as classic fast bowlers. From the outset I have admired his style, which I would willingly watch all day.

Dennis has been blessed with all the attributes required to reach the peak of his particular art form. He is fast-bowling perfection. Like all the truly great pacemen who have been able to go on successfully far longer than they should have been able to, he possesses a fine running action worthy of an Olympic athlete. Couple the way he moves with balance, rhythm, fire in the belly, stamina and a big heart and you are close to greatness. The last piece in the jigsaw is the bowling action, which in the case of Lillee is superb. His action and timing cannot be bettered.

It was during the Australian season of 1978-79 that Lillee amended his running action after a discussion with an Australian athlete. Instead of pumping his arms down his sides, he held them quite high in front of the lower portion of his chest and thus achieved the smoothness which he believes has greatly helped him in the twilight of his career. I am sure he is right. It seems to have enabled him in his approach, which he starts slowly before accelerating into full speed, to be even better balanced when he reaches his delivery stride, and to be higher when he releases the ball.

I would strongly advise any budding quick bowler with a good physique to get hold of a video of Dennis bowling and to study it carefully, because here is a wonderful example of the classical action. His left arm reaches for the sky and points towards fine-leg so that he is sideways-on to the batsman and looking round the left side of his left arm. Then the right arm comes high over the top, swings across close to his body and finishes outside his left leg. Finally there is that sweet, controlled follow-through which reduces the strain on his body.

Although Lillee's speed is derived mostly from his body action, this is by no means its sole contribution. Dennis's ability to swing the ball late, mainly away from the right-hander, to cut it back sharply off the pitch, vary his pace, and to slip in a bouncer without telegraphing his intention all derive from his action.

In terms of figures, Dennis Lillee is the greatest fast bowler ever, but I believe that Ray Lindwall was even better and despite a much lower arm action he swung the ball more. It would have been marvellous to see the two 'Ls' in action together in an era when there were fewer Tests, rather more world-class batsmen about who could afford to ignore balls that pitched outside the off stump, and wickets which were more favourable for batting. At a time, too, when the shine and the seam did not last nearly as long. But that, alas, is impossible.

I particularly admired the determination Dennis displayed after his serious back injury. The way he came back to open the Australian attack, when it was generally believed that he would never bowl again, much less play Test cricket, took courage, the slog of remedial exercises and an enormous amount of sheer hard work. Most cricketers would have given it away, but not Dennis Lillee, which helps explain why he has remained for so long at the top of his profession.

There can be few more exhilarating sights in cricket than watching bowlers like Lindwall, Hall and Lillee in action against top-class batsmen, a combination of excitement and beauty, poetry in motion.

The arrival of Jeff Thomson on the international cricket scene against England was about as explosive as a mortar shell and produced an enormous amount of publicity. In terms of pace he was in the Ray Lindwall class, and though he lacked Ray's control and flowing action, he could make the ball lift more unpleasantly from only just short of a length.

It was my old friend, Richie Benaud, who first told me about 'Thommo'. He had received two telephone calls on the same day telling him about a young bowler who was genuinely quick and had immense potential. Richie was initially somewhat sceptical because Australia tends to claim the arrival of another Bradman every third season and a new Lindwall every other summer. But the praise on this occasion was so high that he felt it deserved further investigation. He went to see Thommo for himself and immediately realised that for once the information was correct. Here was the answer to the Australian dream, an ideal partner for Dennis Lillee – always assuming that Dennis had recovered. It gave Australia extreme pace from both ends; pace which was to prove too much not just for English batsmen, who in 1974-75 wilted under the ceaseless and often painful bombardment, but also for the more talented West Indians the following season.

If anyone doubts the value of very fast bowling at Test level, he has only to examine that 1974-75 series. Australia won the First Test by 166 runs, despite a brave century from Tony Greig, the Second by nine wickets, the Fourth by 171 runs after the Third was drawn, and the Fifth by 163 runs. But the Sixth, when Thommo was injured and did not play and in which Lillee retired after only six overs, England won by an innings and four runs.

Thommo reminds me of Frank Tyson in that for a short period he left a trail of devastation as a result of his exceptional speed. But once he began to lose a little of his edge, initially through injury, and lacking the control and variety of a Lillee, he became just another fast bowler.

Not only is Thommo's style of bowling very different from that of his partner, Lillee, but so is his character. He is essentially a happy-go-lucky individual who loves surfing and sailing and has never given quite the same thought to his cricket, nor to his bowling, as has Dennis. As a result, I cannot help feeling that he has never made as much of his ability as he might have done. For he has the advantage of a build which is absolutely right for fast bowling: tall, athletic, a splendid set of shoulders, and he looks light on his feet. His action is not in the classical mould, but he certainly gets his left shoulder well round and has a long delivery stride. His arm comes from further back than anyone else's I've seen; at times it looks as if he will touch the ground behind him. It is the power and the length of this loop which is primarily responsible for his pace and it puts him into the 'slinger' category, though I would like to emphasise that there has never been anything illegal or suspect about Jeff's bowling. The sling he uses is a straight arm and is entirely legitimate.

Because he is slightly round-arm, Thommo tends to make the ball leave the bat in the air, and sometimes after pitching. One delivery from him which I shall always treasure was the one which completed Graham Gooch's pair at Edgbaston in 1974. It pitched about leg stump and left Graham very fast, even though the wicket was extremely slow. It was one of those times when it would have paid not to have been a fine batsman, because only a very good player would have touched it.

The Lillee-Thomson partnership that destroyed Mike Denness

Jeff Thomson provides a perfect example of a 'slinger's' action
with the low right hand coming from behind the right leg
and the body in an ideal sideways-on position.

In releasing the ball, Thomson has come down hard on a braced
left leg and then swung into a very energetic follow-through
in which both arms play a part.

and company in 1974-75 will go down in history along with those of Gregory and McDonald, Larwood and Voce, and Lindwall and Miller. Although they bowled together on many occasions afterwards, including the series against West Indies in 1975-76, when they played a large part in Australia's winning the rubber with surprising ease, they were never quite so frighteningly effective as when they paired up for the first time to win the Ashes with their fast bowling *blitzkrieg*. – F.S.T.

 When I first saw Dennis Lillee in action, in Australia when England were touring there in 1970-71, he was a novice fast bowler with an exciting run-up and an even more exciting action. His pace was fast, but not frightening, and though his potential was obvious he had not yet acquired the control and variety which were to become such features of his bowling later in his career. This latter aspect was especially noticeable in the final Test at Sydney which decided the Ashes. On his début as captain of Australia, Ian Chappell quite logically put England in to bat on a pitch which, in the early stages, was ideal for accurate seam bowling. It was the type of wicket on which a mature Lillee would have been very anoyed if he hadn't gobbled up at least four batsmen before lunch. Instead it was Australia's spinners, O'Keeffe and Jenner, who did most damage.

In the summer of 1971 Dennis signed on as a professional for Haslingden in the Lancashire League. Although his figures were not all that impressive (68 wickets at 13.85), and certainly did not suggest that an international-class fast bowler was about to emerge, he learnt two important lessons: pace alone on slow wickets was not always enough, and in England it paid to bowl a fuller length than in Australia. Consequently, when he returned a year later at the age of twenty-two as a member of the Australian touring party under Ian Chappell, he quickly established himself as the best paceman in the world by capturing a record-breaking 31 wickets in the five Tests at 17.67 apiece. His bowling was very largely responsible for Australia's success that summer and he was without question the man of the series.

However, it was not merely the wickets he took which caught the imagination of the public, it was his presence. He stood six feet tall with looks, build, hair and exotic moustache straight out of a violent Mexican western. His long, spectacular approach, glorious body action and sheer speed combined with his highly volatile temperament to make him the most exciting fast bowler Australia had sent to these shores since Ray Lindwall. With television catching all his expressions and mannerisms, Dennis became not just another great quickie but a personality. And in an age when commercial sponsorship was becoming the most important feature in professional sport, this meant that Dennis was on his way to fortune as well as fame.

There was drama whenever Lillee bowled because he was sufficiently fast to beat good players, especially those whose re-actions were slowing down – and there were several in that England XI – by sheer speed through the air. His bouncer came close to being lethal, while his yorker, especially at the start of an innings, frequently was. The Lord's Test of that tour will go down in history as Massie's Match – he took 16 wickets with the most remarkable exhibition of sustained swerve bowling I have ever seen – but he would never have obtained such remarkable figures without the hustle and bustle of Dennis at the other end. He gave the batsmen no respite from Massie's swing, although I have never understood why none of the England batsmen tried to counter Massie's threat by playing him from a foot down the pitch, thus automatically reducing the amount of movement.

Apart from Lillee and Massie, the Australian attack was short of penetration and class, which meant that Ian Chappell, who led his side most effectively and astutely, was often forced to employ Dennis as a stock bowler, though he made sure that he did very little bowling outside the Tests. What surprised me was that despite his excessively long run-up, Dennis was still able to sustain his pace. It was a tribute to his physical fitness. But I was also worried, as I watched from the Test Match Special commentary box, by the forty-four paces he walked back to his starting mark. Children tend to imitate the practices of their heroes, and I could see Australia and England breeding a race of marathon runners rather than fast bowlers. I mentioned this on the radio and the outcome was a delightful card, which read: 'Dear Mr Bailey, You are absolutely right. My grandson Shaun, aged three, now runs from eighteen paces before releasing the ball at me from six feet.' It was signed 'Worried Grandma'.

Although very taken by Lillee, the cricketer, during his first triumphant tour of England, I was even more impressed by Lillee, the man, on my next encounter in the West Indies in 1972-73. His successful new-ball partnership with Massie having ended because the latter had suddenly lost his late swing and become just another fast-medium trundler, he remained, despite doubts about his back, the spearhead of the Australian attack and arrived in the Caribbean with the justifiable reputation of being the finest fast bowler in the world. However, in the high-scoring drawn First Test at Sabina Park he looked anything but that as he failed to take a wicket. It was to be his only Test of the tour. His back had gone and it was feared that what should have been a great cricket career was already over.

For the following Test at Bridgetown, Dennis was relegated to the role of spectator, always a depressing experience for a player but even more so in this instance, as Dennis himself must have had doubts about his future. Yet his approach to this most daunting of challenges was exemplary. He was always a fitness fanatic and so, while his team-mates travelled the eight or so miles from the hotel to the ground by bus, he jogged his solitary way to and fro in a tracksuit – not the most comfortable way to travel in Bridgetown. There is no doubt in my mind that the main reason why Dennis was again able to bowl fast was the dedication he put into his recovery programme. A less determined individual would never have made it. What is strange, though, is that the strictly imposed self-discipline required to make himself fit has frequently been absent on the cricket field.

Having recovered from four stressed fractures at the base of his spine, Dennis declared himself fit for the 1974-75 series against England and came back in a blaze of savage glory with Jeff Thomson as his new and equally frightening partner. With some of the most devastating bowling seen for a very long time, this combination proved more than sufficient to sink England. Indeed, they could well have proved too much for a far more formidable and braver batting line-up. Lillee and Thomson provided a classic example of how two genuinely fast bowlers can demoralise as well as dismiss the opposition. However, it would also be true to say that they were helped by umpires who permitted them to send down far too many bouncers, by the majority of the Test pitches being fast and untrustworthy with uneven bounce, and by the gladiatorial atmosphere sustained by crowds baying for blood, chanting 'Lill...Lee, Lill...Lee'. They were also aided by some magnificent close-catching.

During the season a book, *Back to the Mark*, appeared under the name of Dennis Lillee in which he stated that his bouncer was

In the middle of his leap Dennis Lillee is beautifully balanced.
Arms, legs and head are all in the perfect position for
guaranteed complete control.

aimed to hit the batsman with the object of making him wonder whether he was wise to go on batting – always assuming he was in a fit state to continue. In other words, intimidation was the intention. Although this has always been one of the aims of every quickie who has bowled a bouncer, such statements went a long way to making this one of the less pleasant series, especially as, in addition to the physical hostilities, Dennis's audible comments about the batsmen were offensive – as well as puerile. They cried out for a player who was not afraid of his pace and was prepared to laugh at his invective; even to suggest very politely that it was about time he grew up. Unfortunately there was no-one around.

The true greatness of Dennis Lillee as a bowler is reflected in the fact that, when increasing years had taken some of his fire, he remained an outstanding wicket-taker at international level. This was because he had other weapons in addition to speed; the late away-swing, a 'nip-backer', change of pace and of course superb control.

Such skills take years of application and practice, the right temperament and technique to perfect, and without such ground-work most bowlers will never rise above being ordinary. The one exception is the real tearaway quickie. Provided he is sufficiently fast he will worry good batsmen from the outset, while at the same time a high percentage of his loose deliveries will go unpunished. The possession of excessive speed can turn a nonentity into a national hero in the course of a Test match, and never was this more perfectly illustrated than in the case of Jeff Thomson.

The MCC party chosen to tour Australia in 1974-75 under the captaincy of Mike Denness did not inspire much confidence, and one wonders, as one did then, why three Selectors who had never toured Australia as players were entrusted with the job. Neverthe-less the team's initial prospects looked hopeful enough because injury appeared to have ruled out the threat of Dennis Lillee. Nobody had really heard of Jeff Thomson, who had played, with-out success, in one Test against Pakistan the previous season and had been unable to establish himself as a regular member of the New South Wales team.

Jeff at the time was twenty-four years old, six feet tall and had the blonde hair, looks and physique usually associated with the romantic portrait of a surfer. Rather than for his bowling he had become well known in Australia for his juvenile magazine article – ghosted, of course about hurting batsmen. But early in the

1974-75 season he managed to harness his pace sufficiently to become the chief Australian 'hit-man' and to cause mayhem among the English batsmen. Despite Lillee's remarkable recovery, it was newcomer 'Thommo' who was the chief destroyer, and in four and a half Tests he took 33 wickets at just under 18 apiece to ensure that the Australians took the Ashes without being extended. Somewhat typically, he managed to injure himself playing tennis on the rest day of the Fifth Test and so missed the Sixth, which England won in his absence and on the event of Lillee breaking down. However, as Max Walker, Australia's third seamer, picked up eight wickets in England's innings, it is fair to assume that Jeff, had he been fit, would have secured another impressive haul.

Thommo's success in this series stemmed from five different factors. His excessive pace was sufficient to cause errors and fear among batsmen; his slinger's body action, allied to a very strong back, enabled him to make the ball, from only fractionally short of a length, kick to glove and even shoulder height; his splendid physique and his stamina kept him going for long spells without any noticeable loss of speed; he had Dennis Lillee at the other end; and finally, the English batsmen, battered and bewildered by his pace and lift, lost heart and confidence.

The following year it was the turn of the West Indians to wilt under, and finally to capitulate to, the Australian pace bombardment, spearheaded by Lillee and Thomson. However, their highly effective and lethal partnership was nearing its end in international cricket as a result of Thomson's shoulder injury against Pakistan in 1976-77 and Lillee's defection to World Series which, for a few years, was to rob Test cricket of so many of the finest players.

Like all the great fast-bowling duos, Lillee and Thomson were complementary to each other. Dennis is the complete fast bowler, a thinking cricketer who has gone on harvesting wickets long after he lost his fearsome pace. He is the Muhammad Ali of the cricket field, an artist, whereas Thomson is essentially a slugger with a knockout punch but no subtlety. He simply runs up and lets the ball go as fast as he can; but, unlike Lillee, once the pace has gone he will not have much to offer. And if his life at the top was bound to be short, there can be no denying that it has been both colourful and highly successful. In 46 Tests Jeff had blasted out no fewer than 194 batsmen, 22 of them after his recall to the Australian side in 1982-83 following the injuries to Lillee and Alderman.

When Thommo went to England in 1977, without Lillee and

with a shambles of an Australian team, an uneasy mixture of Packerites and non-Packerites, it took him some time to sort out his run – he had had similar trouble in 1975 – and he was still slightly troubled by a shoulder injury. Furthermore he was unable to achieve as much lift on the slower English pitches as he could at home, and yet he still managed to take 23 wickets in the five Tests, again making him the leading wicket-taker. Nevertheless, one gained the impression that Thommo was never really happy away from his native Australian haunts and seemed rather lost both in England and in the Caribbean, where he went with the Australian 'second XI' under Bobby Simpson in the early Packer days. In addition to missing home he must also have missed his mate Lillee and the taste of success to which Australian players had become accustomed before World Series Cricket.

When peace was restored to international cricket in 1979, it seemed that Jeff Thomson was nearing the end of his Test career. In 1981, not chosen for the Australian touring side to England, he signed for Middlesex, an intriguing decision by the champion county and one which, I think, might have proved successful had Jeff not broken down again. He was still quick enough to trouble most England batsmen, as he was to prove when Australia recovered the Ashes in 1982-83.

What I did find somewhat strange was that, after almost a decade of international cricket, Jeff still could not manage a smooth run-up but had to rely on what was no more than a stuttering amble until his last few paces. In addition, he never learnt to get close to the stumps when he released the ball, invariably bowling from the extreme edge of the return crease and frequently even breaking it with his right heel. The fact that he so often escaped being no-balled for this offence was because the umpires were so concerned with where he was putting down his front foot, and what was about to happen at the other end, that they forgot about his back foot. – T.E.B.

West Indian Quickies

West Indian Quickies

Trevor Bailey

Having been lucky enough to visit the Caribbean islands, particularly Barbados, frequently, I have become very fond of the people, sharing their love for the sun, the sea, the beaches, the cricket and, perhaps above all, the laughter which, even in bad times, is never all that far away. In England, we mistakenly tend to group together everybody from the West Indies, failing to appreciate the considerable financial, political, historical, cultural and ethnic differences which exist. It was these differences which were mostly responsible for the failure of that political dream, a West Indian Confederation, although it was obviously a mistake to attempt to build the confederation on what was basically a colonial system, instead of as an association of independent countries.

One aspect of life in which the former British West Indies have so far been able to combine successfully has been cricket, but there are, sadly, signs that this may not continue much longer. If Guyana will not accept Robin Jackman for having coached and played in South Africa, conveniently forgetting that several other members of the England team had offended in the same way, how can they possibly accept Allan Lamb? And what if one island were to 'pardon' those West Indians who toured South Africa in 1982-83? How would the other islands react?

What never ceases to amaze me every time I visit Barbados is the high standard of their cricket and their ability to turn out a seemingly endless supply of fast and lively fast-medium bowlers. The first point was underlined for me a few years ago when one West Indian XI, containing most of their finest cricketers, was playing in World Series Cricket and at the same time another West Indian XI was touring India. Although Barbados is a small island with a population of some 230,000, it had supplied twelve of the players, and yet from those remaining could have been fielded a team which would have been too strong out there for any two English counties, minus their imports, combined. The second point is illustrated by the fact that in 1981 no fewer than six Bajaan-born fast bowlers – Sylvester Clarke, Wayne Daniel, Joel Garner, Ezra Moseley, Hallam Moseley and Hartley Alleyne – were playing first-class cricket in England. And there must be at least another five in Barbados who are good enough at the moment to open the bowling in county cricket.

The young fast bowler in the West Indies will initially, as elsewhere, be made more effective and intimidating by indifferent pitches and frightened batsmen; but not for long. It is so easy to prepare a reasonable wicket on the islands, and there is an abundance of run-hungry batsmen with good eyes and quick reflexes who are only too happy to murder loose bowling irrespective of the pace. Indeed, as the majority of club pitches favour the batsman, and grounds tend to have short boundaries, the apprentice quickie soon appreciates the importance of line and length if he wants to be successful.

In addition to the excitement and the satisfaction of bowling fast, the paceman does enjoy a considerable advantage over the medium and the slow bowlers in the West Indies. The majority of West Indian batsmen, raised on cricket played anywhere with an old tennis ball and when introduced to the proper game finding the pitches faster and truer than those in England, have learnt to hit the ball on the rise from an early age. This, combined with their ability to score runs off good-length bowling with safe, straight-bat strokes, means that the accurate medium-pacer, limited by the amount of movement he can obtain in the air or off the track, regularly comes in for heavy punishment.

The slow bowler, especially the wrist-spinner with a deceptive flight, is often very successful in the Caribbean, but he may be discouraged in his formative years because the short boundaries mean his bowling is forever being lifted out of the ground and the game held up while the ball is found. Furthermore it is difficult to turn the ball on most of the pitches. There have been exceptions, 'those two little pals of mine, Ramadhin and Valentine' for example, but the apprenticeship for a slow bowler is likely to be long and hard, demanding a detached, philosophical view of the game – two characteristics not very plentiful in the Caribbean.

On the other hand, if I were taking a team to the West Indies I would be keen to include a top-class slow bowler. I have always believed that West Indian batsmen, including their finest players, are more vulnerable against this form of attack on good wickets than any other. The strokes played against a spinner with a curving flight are not automatic, and so many of their batsmen cannot resist the challenge of the big hit without first getting their feet right to the pitch of the ball.

The difficulties that West Indian slow and medium-pace bowlers are likely to encounter on their way to gaining a place in an island team stem in part from the fast-bowling tradition that exists there. This began in Victorian and Edwardian times, when black cricketers, like the English professionals, were predominantly bowlers and white West Indians, like the English amateurs, provided most of the runs and all the captains – though the redoubtable 'Cons', father of Sir Learie Constantine, did score the first West Indian century in England. In those early days the majority of the bowling tended to be fast and furious, and visiting teams were delighted to find that there were always plenty of would-be quickies only too willing to bowl at them.

The successful fast bowler enjoys a number of advantages. For one thing, it is possible for him to become an international cricketer in a very short time without having to return the figures expected of a batsman or of most other types of bowler. Even in England, where it normally takes much longer to be selected for Test cricket, the novice fast bowler often finds himself chosen after limited first-class experience, as has happened to Brian Statham, Bob Willis, Graham Dilley and Norman Cowans. For another, there is an enormous demand for genuine fast bowlers. Every team wants at least one, and it is noticeable that many Test series are decided by them.

The fast bowler, too, has crowd appeal. Everyone wants to see him in action and only a great batsman commands more adoration. In the West Indies, cricket provides an escape route to a new social and financial world. The fact that Roberts, Garner, Holding and company have taken a great many wickets, and have made much more money that they could possibly have if they had remained in the Caribbean, has encouraged youngsters with the ability to bowl fast to try to follow in their footsteps.

These, then, are some of the reasons why there are so many West Indian genuinely quick fast bowlers around at the present time. But there is, in my opinion, a more important one.

What have Luther Blissett, John Barnes, Ricky Hill, Mark Chamberlain, Viv Anderson and Cyrille Regis – all selected for the England football squad for an international against West Germany in 1982 – in common with West Indian fast bowlers? The answer is that their parents were from the Caribbean and all are black. They were all born with the natural aptitude, physique and stamina required by high-class footballers and fast bowlers. It seems to me, therefore, that the main reason for the sudden explosion of exciting black footballing talent in England and the surfeit of pace bowlers in the West Indies is ethnographical.

Bowling fast is hard, physical work anywhere, but it is even more demanding in the Caribbean, where the climate is more suited to being 'busy doing nothing' than to thundering up to bowl. The West Indian with African ancestry is physically better equipped to do this than someone of most other races, and it is noticeable that nearly all the best West Indian pacemen have this African connection. It also explains why Barbados turns out a seemingly endless procession of fast men, whereas many of the best batsmen and slow bowlers, such as Rohan Kanhai and Sonny Ramadhin, come from islands with an Indian connection.

Barbados has always been British, indeed was often known as 'Little England', and so the love of cricket there became even more pronounced. Because it was such a small island, when slavery was abolished, indentured servants from Asia were not required to work on the plantations as they were in the case of, say, Guyana. Consequently most Bajaans have their roots in Africa. Though it is not a wealthy island, there is no shortage of food and no cold weather, so poverty in its worse forms has not really existed. The male population has in the main grown up fit and strong with the long powerful arms and legs and broad backs that are ideal for bounding up to the wicket and hurling down a cricket ball at great pace. The only problem is that some of their quickies are so long- and loose-limbed that their bowling action can look suspect, even though it may be quite legitimate. However, it has sometimes seemed to me that batsmen there are a shade too eager to condemn, for on more than one occasion I have made enquiries about a bowler, only to be told 'He sharp, man, but he ping de ball!' This despite the knowledge that no umpire has called him for throwing.

There is nothing new about Barbados being such a prolific nursery for fast bowlers. When I captained a powerful Rothmans Cavaliers team against the island in 1965, their seam attack consisted of Charlie Griffith, 'Prof' Edwards and Gary Sobers. The 'Prof' was certainly as quick as Charlie, possibly a shade quicker, and would have commanded a regular place in most international sides; but he was unlucky to be around when the West Indian pace attack consisted of Hall, Griffith and Sobers. And it cannot have helped to be white.

Although for a long period it was easier for a white man to be picked for West Indies than for a black man, the reverse has applied for some time. Indeed, some very good white cricketers have never been picked, among them Stephen Farmer, who would have revelled in English conditions. Edwards did win selection for the 1968-69 Australasian tour, and though he struggled for wickets in Australia, he was the West Indians' most successful bowler in New Zealand, which rather suggests he would have done very well in England, the wickets in the two countries not being dissimilar.

When we met Barbados a second time on that same Cavaliers tour, we played what was in effect their second XI as many of their top players were required for the forthcoming Test match against Australia in Jamaica. It provided yet another example of the depth of quality of Barbados cricket. We were not at all surprised to find that their three second-string seamers were distinctly quick and hostile, and I was sufficiently impressed by my first glimpse of Keith Boyce, who opened the bowling, to sign him immediately for Essex. Les Ames understandably liked the look of John Shepherd and arranged for him to join Kent. Yet neither player, both of whom were to become outstanding all-rounders in county and then Test cricket, was able to claim a regular place in the Barbados side. It was lucky for Essex and Kent that there happened to be that Test in Jamaica.

Both Boyce and Shepherd illustrated another aspect of West Indian fast bowlers. Being such natural ball players, they usually have a knack of scoring runs, often in a flamboyant and distinctly unconventional way. The hitter-fast bowler has always been a great favourite with spectators, and being a potential match-winner his value has increased with the growing number, and the financial importance, of limited-overs games.

In general, it would be true to say that West Indian fast bowlers have relied more on pace and lift and less on swing and movement off the wicket than their English and Australian counterparts. There has also been a definite tendency by some of them to over-use the bouncer, a particularly bad offender in this respect being Roy Gilchrist, who also employed a much meaner delivery, the deliberate head-high full toss or beamer.

Although Gilchrist, when first picked, was probably the fastest West Indian bowler since Manny Martindale, his international career was short and tempestuous, the result of an explosive temper which resulted in his being sent home in disgrace before the team moved on from India to Pakistan. By then, however, he had taken 26 wickets in four Tests at 17 apiece, and he continued to take wickets and cause controversy in the Lancashire League. I have no hesitation in placing him among the quickest bowlers I have faced, but on a good English wicket he was not especially difficult to play provided one moved into line. He was very straight. It sometimes seemed that there was more than a hint of a jerk in his action, and if he had played in a later era eyebrows might have been raised. On the other hand, as I mentioned earlier in this chapter, it can be difficult to pick some West Indian chuckers.

At first glimpse the action looks almost ideal: right foot parallel to the crease, head coming round over the left shoulder. However, a moment later Charlie Griffith's left foot was still wide of the stumps and his chest was square-on prior to delivery, but then Charlie did not possess that lissome grace of his partner, Wes.

Wes and Charlie

The new-ball partnership of Wes Hall and Charlie Griffith in the sixties was one of the most physically frightening and statistically successful ever, providing another example of the effectiveness of fast bowlers hunting as a pair. Yet when I first heard about the havoc this duo was causing around the English counties in the summer of 1963 I was somewhat intrigued. Not about Wes Hall, whom I had played against on a number of occasions. There was no disputing his speed. No. It was Charlie who surprised me.

When I first came across him in Barbados in 1959-60, Charlie Griffith had been just another, rather ordinary fast-medium bowler. He reminded me somewhat of Derbyshire's Cliff Gladwin; about the same pace, but he didn't move the ball as much and was not nearly such an accomplished bowler. So it didn't make much sense to me when I heard that Charlie was not only knocking over a lot of wickets but was also knocking over a lot of batsmen with his hostile pace. I simply could not imagine the dramatic change that must have taken place in three years, for his bowling had never remotely suggested it was international class when I was in the Caribbean. I was certainly in for a rude awakening when Yorkshire met the West Indians at Middlesbrough and Charlie was in their team.

Ray Illingworth, also on that MCC tour to the West Indies, and I told the rest of the Yorkshire team that they needn't worry about Griffith. He was no more dangerous than a normal county seamer, we said. We won the toss and elected to bat, and I was just settling back in a chair when one of my team-mates said, 'Here, F.S., he's taken an awful long run for a medium pacer'. I looked through the windows, and there to my great surprise was Charlie walking back some thirty yards. I thought to myself he must have been fetching one of those bowling markers which were used sometimes to stop bowlers scarring the turf with their spikes. In the West Indies he had ambled in off about twelve paces. But I was very wrong because Charlie set off at a lumbering trot from that distant mark until, from wide of the crease, he let go a ball which flashed through to be taken by wicket-keeper Allan at chest height. Illy and I looked at each other in utter disbelief. There was a moment's silence in our dressing-room before a voice said, 'Bloody medium-

151

pace. Either you've been taking the micky out of us or you both need white sticks!'

In that match Charlie hit Doug Padgett in the face and John Hampshire, who was a particularly fine player of quick bowling, on the head. John maintains to this day that the reason he was struck on the head was not the pace, though that was very quick, or the length, which was not all that short, but that he simply failed to pick up the ball early enough to take evading action. I know exactly what he means as this happened to me in Australia in 1958-59 when several of the bowlers there had highly suspect actions.

[Untypical Yorkshire modesty has prevented Fred from mentioning that Yorkshire beat the West Indians by 111 runs, largely through the efforts of one F.S.T. who scored 55 (after Yorkshire had been 95 for six) and 20 not out, had match figures of 10 for 81, and held two catches. – T.E.B.]

Later that same summer, in a Test match at The Oval, I had a similar experience to John's. Although the light was not very good, and the new ball had just been taken, I had no difficulty in seeing Wes Hall from the Vauxhall End. However, in the next over I found myself facing Charlie from the Pavilion End, and when I managed to hit him for four, he gave me the look that most fast bowlers reserve for batsmen who have the temerity to strike them to the boundary. 'Fred', I said to myself, 'this next ball is going to be a bit quick'. And it was. He ambled up, his left foot landed wide of the crease and I saw his arm come over. But as I went through the motions of pushing slightly forward, I thought to myself he hadn't released the ball. He had though, as I realised when my middle stump flew out of the ground. I simply could not believe it. It was the only time in my life that I never saw the ball. I was so annoyed, not at getting out but because, as a result of his action, I had been unable to pick up the ball. Had it been directed at my head, and not the wicket, I might not have been around to relate the story. I don't mind how fast anyone bowls provided you can see the ball from his hand, and this was not always the case with Charlie.

Wes Hall, on the other hand, never sparked off a moment of controversy. He was, to me, easily the finest fast bowler the West Indies have ever produced. He stood over six feet tall and was so magnificently proportioned that he could have been designed by a precision engineer.

I first encountered him at Bradford, when the 1957 West Indians played Yorkshire, and I immediately liked what I saw; the action and the rhythmical approach to the wicket. At close of play our wicket-keeper, Jimmy Binks, remarked to me, 'This fellow Hall's a bit quick, F.S. It wouldn't surprise me to see him in their Test side before the end of the tour.' This was fair comment, even though Wes had been bowling from the old football stand end – a considerable handicap. No fast bowler ever wanted to bowl from that end because it meant running up the hill. The pitch always seemed at least 23 yards long by the time you got into your delivery stride. Because he always seemed to have the right word for any situation, it was probably Emmott Robinson who said that bowling from the football stand end 'was like running up the cellar steps with a barrel of beer on your back'.

Wes did not make the West Indian Test team that summer. He had to wait for their tour to India and Pakistan in 1958-59, when in eight Tests he captured 46 wickets at 18 apiece, and from that moment he was an automatic choice. Consequently, on my next meeting with Wes, in the Caribbean in 1959-60, we were the main strike bowlers for our respective sides in a very high-scoring five-Test series which England won one-nil. Wes shared the new ball with Chester Watson, who was a much better bowler than is often realised outside the West Indies, and they formed a very good partnership.

It was easy to see why Wes had developed from a good prospect into a world-class paceman. In addition to increased pace through the air, he had acquired a classical fast bowler's action with his left shoulder coming right round so that it pointed down the wicket at the batsman. This enabled him to move the ball away from the right-hander and, combined with his speed, was one of the main reasons why he was West Indies' leading wicket-taker with 22 victims against a powerful England batting line-up. (Five of our players averaged over 40.)

The Wes Hall run-up was one of the longest I have seen, but unlike the marathon excursions of subsequent imitators, many of whom are no more than fast-medium, it was also one of the most graceful I have had the pleasure to witness. He reminded me of a train leaving a station: that slow, deliberate start gradually building up to full speed as he approached his delivery stride. This incorporated the timing, balance and rhythm required to propel the ball at a pace sufficient to alarm even the brave.

Wes really enjoyed cricket and life in general. He possessed a great sense of humour, an infectious laugh, loved a story and could always tell one against himself. One such involved that breathtaking draw in the historic Lord's Test of 1963 when Colin Cowdrey had to come in to bat at number eleven with a broken arm. In the course of the last innings, throughout which Wes bowled virtually unchanged, England were saved by Brian Close, who made 70 in just under four hours and was repeatedly hit by the West Indian quick bowlers. Afterwards Brian proudly showed his bruises to the photographers, and the graphic mementoes of his heroic stand upset some England followers when the pictures appeared in the newspapers next day.

The West Indians played Essex shortly after that match, and before the start of play Wes was opening his mail. He read one letter, which also contained a photo of the bruised and battered Close, and began to laugh, a sound sufficiently loud to quieten even a West Indian dressing-room. Asked what was so funny, Wes read out part of the letter which went something like 'you big, ugly black bear, have you seen what you have done to poor Brian Close?' Then he turned to his bowling partner and said, 'Hey, Charlie, they've sent this letter to the wrong fellow!' – F.S.T.

 Apart from their both being Bajaans and fast bowlers, it would be hard to find two cricketers more dissimilar than Wes Hall and Charlie Griffith. Yet their many differences were one of the reasons why they formed such an effective new-ball partnership.

Wes was built on the lines of those superb thoroughbred horses he loved so much and used to ride as a kid; a magnificent black stallion, lean, lithe, and exciting to watch just moving towards the starting gates. Tall, graceful, wide-shouldered and narrow-hipped, Wes simply glided over the ground during his long, spectacular run-up from a mark near the edge of the boundary. Nobody ever worried or complained about the length of his approach because it was one of the most beautiful sights in the game. Charlie, too, was a big man, but with the ideal build for a professional bouncer. His presence alone would have been enough to stop trouble. His ambling run-up exuded all the menace and purpose of a tank moving into battle.

Wes seemed to flow into a high classical action and a glorious follow-through. The outcome was exceptional speed, a natural away swing, lift from only just short of a length and the occasional

Wes Hall, at full steam ahead, flows out of his delivery stride into a follow-through
as full of grace and intent as the spectacular run-up which preceded it.
Note the position of the head and the straight right arm.

break-back. His pace was never less than very fast, and on occasions pure black lightning. Unquestionably he was among the quickest and most magnificent fast bowlers cricket has ever seen. In sharp contrast Charlie lumbered into a powerful, open-chested, rather constricted action with which he propelled the ball at a lively, but hardly lethal, speed. His command of line and length was always good, but he would never have been more than a competent pace bowler had he not possessed three other weapons that made him feared more by opposing batsmen than was his partner, Wes.

In between plugging steadily away at just over fast-medium, Charlie had the ability to unleash either a mean bouncer or a deadly yorker. Both were genuinely quick and had the knack of either hitting the stumps or the unfortunate recipient, who was usually unable to detect the increase in speed until it was too late. He also possessed a slower ball which was extremely well disguised and difficult to pick. Not surprisingly, many batsmen, among them as good a judge as the late Ken Barrington, maintained that Charlie's ability to produce this sudden extra pace, or the splendid slower ball, come about because he threw those deliveries. True, he had many of the characteristics of a thrower, including the splayed left foot and the early opening up and dropping away of his left shoulder, but I was never able to make up my mind. This despite batting against him on many occasions, and also having him as a member of the West Indian team which I managed for Rothmans during their short tour to England.

There can be no doubt that Charlie was unlucky to find himself in the middle of a bitter controversy over the legitimacy of his action. Had he been bowling in the fifties it would have gone unquestioned, for he was far less suspect than, for example, Cuan McCarthy of South Africa, Peter Loader of England or his fellow-West Indian, Gilchrist. His misfortune was to arrive on the scene shortly after the 'throw-draggers' and the chuckers of Australia and England had been banned from the game. Although this clean-up had been necessary, it did lead to something of a witch hunt. The Australians in particular seemed to see throwers everywhere. In Barbados, I discovered that those Bajaan players who thought Charlie was a 'pinger' did not mention it in his presence and tended to be those who played against him for other clubs.

In character, as in their bowling, Wes and Charlie were entirely different. Wes was a laughing extrovert who bubbled with life. On one occasion I drove him across England and he never drew breath, telling me about his boyhood in Barbados, how he wanted to become a jockey, his days as a wicket-keeper – he did not take up fast bowling until he left school – and his passion for horses, the animals not the betting. But Charlie was quiet, inclined to be moody, and was suspicious – partly as a result of the throwing controversy, I imagine – of anyone white. Today, however, it is a different story. Charlie has mellowed with the years and is great fun.

I first noticed the change in the late sixties when I was talked into playing in an exhibition game by some friends. They told me it was a little friendly game against a touring party from Ireland, which turned out to be a distinctly useful West Indian touring party led by Charlie! The game was played on an unpleasant green wicket and Charlie was still distinctly lively. Only this Charlie chuckled when the ball lifted sharply and there was no meanness of spirit. He is a man I look forward to meeting whenever I go back to Barbados, which has become almost a second home for me.

Something that Wes and Charlie had in common was their love of batting. Both not only were firmly convinced of their ability in this department, but each believed he was better than the other – as is often the case with fast-bowling partners. Wes and Charlie batting together provided a delightful cricket cameo, especially as their calling was often optimistic and always loud.

I first played against Wes Hall when he toured England in 1957 with John Goddard's West Indians as the junior member of their three specialist pace bowlers, the others being Roy Gilchrist and Tom Dewdney. It may seem strange, in the light of recent events, to think of West Indies going on tour with only three quickies, especially as Wes was very much a novice and was never seriously considered for a Test. In fact he sent down less than 300 overs during the visit. However, it has to be remembered that the tourists were looking to Ramadhin and Valentine to repeat their earlier triumph, that Frank Worrell was a more than useful new-ball bowler, Denis Atkinson was a very good seam-bowling all-rounder, Sobers and 'Collie' Smith were spin-bowling all-rounders, and that Goddard himself was also an all-rounder. At that time Wes possessed a fine action and his pace was little more than fast-medium, but he learnt a great deal. It certainly came as no surprise when he became an automatic member of the West Indian new-ball pair during the 1958-59 tour to India and Pakistan.

By the time Wes made his second tour to England, under the

captaincy of Frank Worrell in 1963, he had established himself as a world-class fast bowler and he enjoyed the luxury of having a high-quality bowler at the other end, the redoubtable Charlie; not forgetting Gary Sobers as first change. West Indies won the series fairly comfortably, with Charlie emerging as their leading wicket-taker with 32 wickets, exactly twice as many as Wes.

The manner and the ease with which the West Indians were annihilating both the counties and our national side caught the imagination of the public, and so a vast crowd assembled at Southchurch Park to watch them play Essex. We bowled them out for just over 200, and that would have been considerably less if we had held our catches. Then my side found itself confronted by Wes and Charlie on a pitch which had been freshened by rain. Our very talkative opening batsman, Gordon Barker, a good, experienced player of pace bowling, had spent hours that summer telling us just how he would deal with Wes and Charlie, but his intent exceeded the execution. He holed out off, of all things, a slow full toss in the first over, the first of five wickets by Wes in 33 deliveries for 14 runs. We were dismissed for a miserable 56, and saved from complete ignominy by teenager Keith Fletcher, who made an impressive 29. Wes and Charlie bowled unchanged, and following on we found ourselves struggling at 38 for four before Keith, again showing his potential and ability against fast bowling, and I managed to avoid a second débâcle. We were finally rescued by what *Wisden* called 'a veritable deluge'.

My abiding memory of Wes is facing him as captain of the Rothmans Cavaliers at Sabina Park, which is a very small ground. Wes, who was playing at that time for Jamaica, seemed to start his gallop up to the stumps from a spot underneath the press box, and I watched him approach with admiration, and not a little anxiety, while the gold chain round his neck swung free. As he released the ball I played a somewhat tentative half-cock off my front foot and was struck a very painful, numbing blow on my left thigh-pad. Down I went, wondering whether I would require a runner. But I needn't have worried. I got to my feet to discover I'd been adjudged lbw; or to be more accurate, thigh-before-wicket.

How did Wes and Charlie compare with that volatile West Indian opening pair of the thirties, Learie Constantine and Manny Martindale? It is impossible for me to provide an accurate assess-ment based on personal experience, because I did not see either bowling in his prime. In his early days Learie was decidedly bouncer happy, and there was no doubt that both were very fast and hostile, as is illustrated by the fact that in 1933, the summer following the Bodyline series in Australia, they were able to bowl an effective version of bodyline on English pitches against a strong England batting side. The English batsmen on the receiving end (although Jardine played it bravely and well) were sufficiently impressed by their pace to agree that this form of attack should be outlawed. Their pace has also been confirmed for me by two of the best judges in the game, Bob Wyatt and Leslie Ames.

During the war I had the good fortune to play with and against Learie Constantine in a number of matches, and against Manny on a couple of occasions. Although both were well past their best, and the blistering pace had long since departed, there was still much to admire. Age can blur, but it cannot hide genuine class.

Learie was really made for limited-overs cricket; a very fast bowler, a flamboyant hitter rather in the style of Keith Boyce, but with an even better eye, and a superbly athletic, all-purpose fieldsman at a time when the general standard was not as high as it is today. His all-round record in 18 Test matches in somewhat disappointing, and indeed would be more impressive if his batting and bowling averages could be switched round. It would be fair to say that he proved a far more effective bowler at international level than a batsman, for he relied too much on cross-bat strokes and hitting across the line to score heavily against the English and Australian international bowlers. In League cricket, though, he was frequently magic.

My most vivid memory of playing cricket with Learie was in a British Empire XI match during the war when I found myself batting with him. The opposing fast – by club standards – bowler dropped one slightly short outside Learie's off stump, and I am not sure who was more surprised, the bowler or myself, when he cut it for an almost flat six just over an astonished cover's head.

As bowlers should concentrate on hitting a particular stump, this is more likely to occur if they can keep their eyes as firmly fixed on the target as is possible. Learie, however, ignored this principle, tossing his head back so violently as he moved into his delivery stride that one wondered at times why it didn't come off. His pace when I played him was just above medium, but he did possess one of the most cleverly disguised really slow balls that I have seen. It must have taken him much time and work to perfect, but it must also have brought him many wickets

From Larwood to Lillee

Emanuel 'Manny' Martindale was short for a fast bowler, about five feet eight, but he had a neat, compact, positive action following a pleasing straight approach. When I played against him he was a very accurate seamer of just over medium-pace, moving the ball a little in the air and cutting the odd one back off the seam. It was easy to imagine how fast he must have been in his prime. – T.E.B.

Gary Sobers

Gary is a member of that small group – growing because of the ever-increasing number of Test matches – of players who took more than 200 wickets in international cricket. But what makes him so very different from the others, apart from his also being a world-class batsman, is that his 235 wickets were obtained using three entirely different styles; seam, orthodox finger-spin and wrist-spin. In many respects his unique ability to capture wickets at international level with three contrasting forms of bowling is even more remarkable than his genius as a batsman. The game has never seen a more complete bowler, or a more complete cricketer.

Of his three styles, Gary was most feared as a fast left-arm seam and swing bowler, although he did not start to use this method until he had established himself in Test cricket as a slow left-armer and a great batsman. It was in English league cricket that he first began to develop as a pace bowler, finding that he could pick up more wickets that way than with left-arm spin. His speed stemmed from a classical sideways-on action with his head looking over the outside of a high right arm, a brisk, brief, rhythmic approach and a poetic follow-through. He discovered in the nets that he was faster off a few paces than the majority of recognised bowlers off their full runs and initially his success stemmed from pace.

It was the late Sir Frank Worrell, when he became captain of West Indies, who realised how formidable his team would become if Gary could also take on the vital role of third seamer. Although he did bowl some seam in India for the West Indians, it was not until the 1960-61 tour to Australia that he showed himself to be a quick bowler of Test calibre. To his pace and his awkward line away from the right-hand batsman he had added the subtleties of seam and swing, and in particular the ability to swerve the ball from on and outside the right-hander's off stump back into him. He managed several times to trap Geoff Boycott leg-before with this delivery to emphasise further its enormous value to left-arm swing bowlers.

How fast was Gary? In his early days he was distinctly quick, and he himself reckoned that when he chose to slip himself, which he did from time to time, he was capable of the odd delivery which was as fast as anything from Wes Hall or Charlie Griffith. He certainly swung the ball more than those two, which is why he sometimes opened with the new ball. In the second innings of the Headingley Test of 1963, for example, Gary struck in his opening over and went on to capture three of the first four wickets.

Although he had a highly respectable bouncer, which he did not over-use, Gary was, rather like Botham, essentially an attacking bowler who believed in keeping the ball up to the bat. He might be driven to the boundary, but if the ball moved late there was the real chance of a wicket. Towards the end of Gary's career, after his second knee operation, his pace dropped to around fast-medium.

His career as a chinaman and googly bowler was brief. He bowled it seriously for less than five years, so it is impossible to judge how good he might have become had he had more time to concentrate on what is the most demanding of all styles of bowling. Many maintain that it takes a minimum of a decade to master. Nevertheless, Gary, as left-arm wrist-spinner, took wickets regularly at international and Australian state level to illustrate that he was a most accomplished performer.

Like his seam bowling, his wrist-spin really began in the Lancashire League, although he had been able to spin the ball viciously as a small boy. It was natural that he would experiment with the occasional chinaman in the nets and he was quick to note the almost hypnotic effect it had on the majority of club players. Consequently he began to slip in a few during League matches, obtaining highly satisfactory results. Although it is possible to combine the chinaman with orthodox finger-spin at club level, class batsmen will play it easily unless it is supported by a well-concealed googly. Gary learnt how to disguise and pitch such a delivery in a remarkably short time, so that in under two seasons he was capturing wickets in first-class cricket as a wrist-spinner. It is feasible for a leg-break bowler to succeed without a googly, provided he has a useful top-spinner, but no left-arm wrist-spinner has yet proved effective at international level without a googly.

The appeal of wrist-spin bowling to Gary was obvious. It represented a new challenge, was an essentially attacking form of bowling, and there are few, if any, more satisfying moments in bowling than deceiving a batsman with a googly on a perfect pitch. However, such an art-form is not without its demands, and Gary's life as a Test-class chinaman and googly bowler effectively ended

As with everything he did, Gary Sobers bowled fast in the classical manner: sideways-on action, eyes looking over the shoulder, the body rocking back at the end of an easy, economical approach which moved into a beautiful follow through.

in 1966 when his shoulder gave way under the strain of bowling the googly – by no means an unusual complaint for wrist-spinners, especially those with high arm actions.

Gary gained his first cap for West Indies as an orthodox slow left-arm bowler who could also bat, and he bowled this way intermittently throughout his cricket career. But it was his least successful and certainly his least spectacular method. On good pitches, especially in Test matches, the slow left-armer is largely employed as a stock bowler; someone to keep the batsmen quiet in the hope that they will eventually make a mistake. Although he could, and on occasions did, do this, it was an approach which never much appealed to Gary. His figures as an orthodox left-arm slow bowler in his first Test, 28.5–9–75–4, suggest that he possessed the ability to have become a great bowler in this style, an opinion reinforced when, at Brisbane in 1968-69, after a few overs of pace, he took six Australian second-innings wickets for 73 in a marathon spell of orthodox spin to win the match.

Viewed statistically, Gary's wickets in international cricket were quite expensive – 34 apiece. One reason for this, the most important, was that most of his Tests were played on good batting wickets and mainly against good, very good and sometimes great batsmen. He never encountered a batting side as weak as, say, the 1981 Australians; or even worse, Pakistan minus their Packerstanis in 1978. Only one Pakistani made over fifty in the three-Test series, which made picking up wickets little more than a formality! Furthermore Gary was always an attacking bowler. His two chief styles provided the main support either for the pace of Hall and Griffith or the off-spin of Lance Gibbs. As a result, he was the one who had to operate up the hill or into the wind; or if the pitch was taking spin, he would have second choice of ends. It is also worth remembering that, unlike most bowlers who usually enjoy the chance to put their feet up in the pavilion, Gary spent an enormous amount of time at the crease making runs.

Towards the end of his career, he had not only lost some of his pace and was troubled by a suspect knee, but also the West Indian attack was on the decline. Therefore, as well as his own reduced effectiveness, he was also having to bowl too much in conditions that were anything but helpful to bowlers.

Here are just two examples of why Gary was, after Alan Davidson and Bill Johnston, the best left-arm pace bowler since the Second World War. In the first innings of the Fifth Test against Australia in 1960-61, Gary came on to bowl – slow at first – when the score was 124 for none and did not come off until the Australians were 335 for nine. He took the second new ball and finished with 44–7–120–5; remarkable figures when one takes into account the Melbourne heat, the quality of the opposition, the placid pitch and the fact that he was bowling eight-ball overs.

Another great spell which especially pleased Gary was for the Rest of the World against England at Lord's, always one of his favourite grounds, in 1970. Bringing himself on as first change he proceeded to take six for 21 on a cloudy day as England were dismissed for 127. He followed this up with an innings of 183, otherwise he would probably have taken more than a couple of wickets in the second innings. – T.E.B.

It is difficult to say anything about Gary Sobers which has not already been said, but there was one occasion when his versatility really surprised me. I had seen him in action both in England and the West Indies, and while listening to an account of the Test match between West Indies and Australia, in Melbourne, I heard that Gary had opened the bowling. My immediate reaction was that the tourists must have had injuries for this to occur. I had seen Gary bowling slow left-arm orthodox and chinamen and googlies during my last tour to the West Indies in 1959-60, but it had never entered my head that he would ever become a fine new-ball bowler. But then that was Gary. I reckon he could have turned himself into a great wicket-keeper if he had wanted to.

When I saw Gary in his new role of third seamer for West Indies, I was immediately impressed. Like everything else he did, he made it look good, easy, elegant and graceful. His run-up, sideways-on action and follow-through all flowed together with the perfection of a high-class golfer's grooved swing. Like Alan Davidson, he was able to swerve the ball in to the right-hand batsman, only he did it faster and tended to move it even more. This way he dismissed a large number of very good players adjudged leg-before.

Whether batting, bowling or fielding, Gary was a law unto himself. He was the most complete cricketer there has ever been, and I have admired him enormously both as a player and as a man. What few people know is that I once had the pleasure of opening the bowling with him for Yorkshire. My county went on a marvellous tour of Canada, America and Bermuda, and Gary was brought out to play against us in Bermuda. However, he decided he would rather like to play for us, because he tended to play and think about the game in the same way as a Yorkshireman. (There is a great deal of talk about carefree, calypso cricket in the West Indies which is pure fantasy. The West Indian cricketer, especially if he comes from Barbados, may laugh more, but he plays the game just as hard and as ruthlessly as the toughest Yorkshireman.) The outcome of Gary's decision was that he and I took the new ball for Yorkshire in Bermuda. I can tell you something. I could have done with him as my regular partner. Not only was there the natural contrast of left and right, but we would never have quarrelled over ends. Our requirement regarding which way the wind was blowing across the pitch was completely different.

On his Test début in 1954 I slipped Gary a bouncer. Although he ducked, it went close to pinning him, and he immediately said that he would not duck again. He never did, because it meant taking his eye off the ball, which he never had to because he always had so much time.

On my next tour to the West Indies we sometimes used the ploy of stationing two men back on the leg boundary for the catch. This now seems to be standard practice against all batsmen who hook or try to hook. It did not work with Gary because, even though he was a devastating hooker, he reckoned this shot against a fast bowler was an unnecessary risk. He would simply sway inside and watch the ball go through to the 'keeper. On the other hand, if there was only one man back on the fence, he was only too happy to accept the challenge of the bouncer and he very seldom holed out.

Like all bowlers, I found Gary very hard to dismiss. The best chance for a quickie was in the first few overs just outside his off stump. On one occasion I bowled him by going round the wicket, but as he had already made a double-century this tactic might be thought to have been tried rather too late. The ball had pitched in the rough and kept very low. Still I was surprised when Gary said afterwards that he did not think it was right for a fast bowler to bowl into the rough from round the wicket. Mind you, he had not at that time joined the seamer's brigade. When he did, I have no doubt that his view changed, as he regularly exploited the worn patches from over the wicket at both right- and left-hand batsmen. – F.S.T.

The Caribbean Pace Quartet

Although there are indications that they could be on the decline, West Indies for the past seven or eight years have been the best team in the world at both Test and limited-overs cricket. What would you put down as the main cause of their domination?

I reckon there are four reasons why the West Indians have been the undisputed world champions: Andy Roberts, Mike Holding, Colin Croft and Joel Garner. Together they have been the vital factor. And they have always had someone like Malcolm Marshall or Sylvester Clarke ready to step in.

.E.B. What makes your assessment especially interesting is that, although there's nothing new about a four-pronged pace attack, it used to be considered a recipe for disaster. It offended the basic principle of a well-balanced attack, which was the aim of every captain. For example, Jardine in 1932-33 made one of his few mistakes as captain when he went into the Second Test at Melbourne with no less than five quick bowlers – Harold Larwood, Bill Voce, 'Gubby' Allen, Bill Bowes and Wally Hammond. The outcome was England's only defeat of the series.

F.S.T. We did exactly the same thing in the First Test against West Indies at Sabina Park in 1953-54. We wrongly supposed that the opposition was suspect against pace and took the field with Brian Statham and myself, plus you and Alan Moss. The result was a heavy and painful defeat.

T.E.B. I must confess that I thought we'd learnt our lesson at Sabina and so was flabbergasted when Godfrey Evans told me in the hotel lift on the evening before the First Test in Brisbane a few years later that we had made the same mistake again. Our attack then consisted of Frank Tyson, Alec Bedser, Brian Statham and myself, with possible support provided by the fairly unpredictable wrist-spin of Denis Compton and the even more improbable non-turning off-breaks of Bill Edrich. Bill, if my memory serves me right, had sent down three overs on the tour.

Though his left arm is lower than the textbooks recommend and his body slightly
open, Andy Roberts's right arm comes over high and so enables him to move the
ball through the air and off the seam. A short bustling approach
and compact body action allow him to bowl with tight control.

What made this selection seem even more incredible, both at the time and in retrospect, was that we had in our party two well-above-average spinners in Bob Appleyard and Johnny Wardle. We lost by an innings and plenty, and from that moment I became convinced of the necessity, on a good wicket, of having a balanced attack – until the arrival of the West Indian pace quartet. Why do you think they have upset my theory and have been so successful?

.T. In my opinion, their success stems from two things. Firstly, they are all fine fast bowlers. Secondly, they are completely different in style, which gives us a contradiction in terms, a balance of pace. To illustrate what I mean, let me analyse them.

Holding is slightly built for a fast bowler and is therefore injury prone, despite a long, silky run-up which flows into a beautiful action. Although he mainly uses a very lengthy approach, he can still be very fast off a much shorter one, but that long run-up does help him to produce great pace without putting too much strain on a build more suitable for a track athlete than a boxer. He was, of course, a very fine runner and his main weapon is sheer speed through the air.

Roberts has a comparatively short, straight bustle up to the stumps. Although his action is slightly open-chested and his left arm is lower than the textbook advocates, his right arm is high. He is able to bowl a very effective late out-swinger, as well as the ball which nips back sharply off the seam. His success comes from speed, combined with excellent control and the ability to change his pace without changing his action. He is a complete fast bowler, which is why he has been able to retain his place in the West Indian team, despite having lost a little of his initial speed and despite considerable pressure from younger rivals.

In addition to a well-disguised slower ball, Roberts possesses two bouncers, which cannot be picked before the ball has been released. This was perfectly demonstrated in a World Series match when he fed Barry Richards with a bouncer which allowed this great batsman to sway back and cut the ball down past third man. The next ball landed on almost exactly the same spot – which was carefully examined by the player before he returned to the pavilion – but this bouncer gloved Barry while he was still swaying back, because it was at least a yard faster. And these two had been team-mates for Hampshire for some years, so if anyone could have picked the difference it should have been Barry.

Croft's long amble up to the wicket takes him into a high, open and ugly action, the most intriguing feature of which is the sudden swing out to the left, with the result that he brings his left foot down probably wider on the crease than any other bowler. This means he automatically slants the ball into the batsman. However, the angle is so wide that to hit the leg stump with a good-length delivery, he needs to pitch well outside the off stump – a fact which does not always appear to have been appreciated by umpires. Everything about the bowling of Croft goes against the textbook, especially his action, which some consider questionable. The fact that he has not been no-balled for throwing in either county or Test cricket indicates that the umpires have not had any doubts, or alternatively suggests that they were not prepared to cause another major controversy.

Although Croft is far removed from the classical fast bowler, there is no doubting his effectiveness. His unusual line, combined with the lift he is able to obtain on even an unresponsive pitch, makes him difficult and different to face. In addition, he is able to keep bowling for long and usually very economical spells. However, perhaps his greatest asset is that, despite bowling from very wide of the crease, he still makes the odd ball hold its own. This is remarkable, and given the latest lbw Law which forces batsmen to play at deliveries they would once have been content to leave, you have a major reason for his success.

Garner might be termed, in a cricket sense, a freak. He looks more like a basketball player than a fast bowler. For a big man, standing six feet eight, he is extremely athletic, as can be seen in the way he brings off catches close to the ground. He has realised that he can never hope to be a tearaway fast bowler, because he has the wrong build, so he bowls at lively fast-medium, swinging the ball in the air and sometimes moving it off the seam. And because of his height, he does make the ball bounce. The workhorse of the foursome, he never gives anything away and is the most likely to cause a collapse when the batting side appears to be on top.

What makes batting against Garner so difficult is picking up his length which, because of his height, is different from that of all the other bowlers. His yorker is not only steeper and harder to dig out, but his good-length ball frequently has to be fended down from about waist high. Consequently, though it is not as fast as that of his colleagues, he can afford to pitch his bouncer further up.

While Joel Garner's action might not please all the purists,
it suits him and his build, which is the important factor.
At fast-medium pace he is a more difficult prospect than bowlers of faster pace;
a shock, stock and brake bowler.

T.E.B. I maintain that one of the greatest, possibly the greatest, piece of sustained fast bowling it has been my privilege to witness was by Michael Holding in the 1976 Test at The Oval. To appreciate the full significance of this performance, it is first necessary to realise that it was achieved on an absolute featherbed, exactly like the one on which, the previous year, England had followed on with a deficit of 341 runs and had put together 538 runs in their second innings against Lillee, Thomson and Walker in their prime. The Oval wicket was so placid that the West Indians scored 687 for eight in their first innings and 182 without loss from only 32 overs in the second innings. Bob Willis, England's main strike bowler, was forced to resort to a field that would have been over-defensive for the last overs of a limited-overs game.

It is fascinating, and revealing, to examine the figures of the other fast and medium-fast bowlers of both teams in that match. For England, Willis took one wicket for 121 runs in 22 overs, Selvey none for 111 in 24 overs, Woolmer none for 74 in 14 overs and Greig, who mixed seam and off-spin in the course of his 36 overs, two for 107. For West Indies, Roberts captured one wicket for 139 runs in 40 overs, Holder three for 106 in 41.5 overs, Daniel none for 30 in 10 overs and King one for 39 in 13 overs.

England scored 435 in their first innings, despite Holding's remarkable analysis of 33–9–92–8, which suggested that, as the follow-on had been averted, a draw was a near certainty. However, such thinking failed to take into account the speed of Holding, who in England's second innings produced figures of 20.4–6–57–6 to bowl his side to an unlikely victory of 231 runs. It was a supreme example of what sheer speed can achieve on even the most perfect pitch. I do not believe any other bowler in the world at that time could have turned in that performance; indeed later, when he became more experienced, I doubt whether Holding himself would have had the mental and physical drive needed to turn in those truly remarkable figures.

In 1981, on a much livelier pitch in Barbados, Holding also produced two of the fastest overs I have seen. In one he removed Boycott and in the other Botham, the two main batting threats. It was one of the very few occasions when I was rather glad that I was no longer playing Test cricket.

Although genuine speed, which worries all batsmen and frightens some, is the first essential for a young quick bowler, those who also have a grooved action will find that they can continue to take wickets at the highest class when they have lost some of their pace. Lindwall, yourself, Lillee and Roberts all come into this category, compensating with increased control and guile for the slight loss of speed through the air. I believe that you, Fred, were a better and certainly a much more complete bowler in your late twenties than when you were blasting them out in your early twenties.

Roberts is a thoughtful quickie who is eager to capitalise on a batsman's weakness. He is helped by a balanced run-up which takes little out of him and allows him to camouflage his changes of pace, which is largely derived from powerful shoulders, arms and back. What has always pleased me about his bowling is that when a batsman fails to make contact, there is every chance the ball will hit the stumps. Furthermore he controls himself much better than so many of his contemporaries. His anger smoulders, rather than bursts into flames.

In sharp contrast to Roberts, Croft has not acquired the same self-control. He may detest all batsmen, but he does make it rather too obvious. It has always seemed to me that the reason he did not take as many wickets as he should have for Lancashire, in his first spell with them, was that he appeared more interested in hitting the batsmen than the stumps. When I was batting against a bowler whose main concern was to knock me out rather than to take my wicket, I reckoned he had lost the initiative. None the less, Croft's unusual line, combined with his pace and hostility, makes him a formidable opponent. He is never more dangerous than when the batting side, if not in command, at least appear secure. In that situation he is liable to produce a ball which holds its own and takes the outside edge.

Garner is a magnificent bowler, the ideal third seamer in any side; both a match-winner and a stock bowler. In addition to having to contend with his bounce and his control, the poor batsman has to pick out a ball from well above the normal sight-screen from a whirl of gangling arms and legs.

When teaching a small boy to play back, I believe that the coach should throw the ball from a kneeling position. In that way he is able to provide a trajectory similar to what the pupil will encounter in a match. If he bowls at him from a full height, it is rather frightening and in fact is not unlike what adult batsmen experience when they face the 'Big Bird'.

F.S.T. Another important reason for the West Indian success has been

Speed through the air is Michael Holding's principal asset, its source being the
long, fluid run-up that flows almost unnoticed into a graceful jump and a
running-through action. Fitness and timing are vital for such a bowler and
any injury can disrupt his rhythm.

their very slow over-rate. On their last visit to England, in 1980, it was not unusual for them to send down under thirteen overs per hour, which meant that the second new ball was still not due after a full day's play. While this robs the spectators of a great deal of cricket, it does have both practical and tactical advantages.

The practical advantage is that none of the four fast bowlers takes too much out of himself, being required to bowl under twenty overs in a full day. It also means that the captain always has two fresh bowlers at his command to slip in at new batsmen. Furthermore, his bowlers will still be fit and raring to go on the second day. It will be appreciated that the fast bowler who sends down thirty or more overs on the first day may have lost a little of his edge when he has to start again.

The tactical plus is that the batting side is automatically slowed down to such an extent that the odds must be on a draw should the West Indian attack fail to dismiss the opposition twice. Assuming that the opposing batting side averages three runs per over, not bad going against high-quality bowling, they will still not reach 200 in six hours. A total of over 400 will effectively take up two-fifths of the match. Unless West Indies can be forced to follow on, which on a good wicket and with their batting line-up is not too likely, a draw may become probable as early as the second day. And while it is true that Clive Lloyd normally employs attacking fields to support his pacemen, he is quite capable of shutting up the game still further by using run-saving, rather than wicket-taking, placements should it suit him.

.E.B.   In addition to finding under seventy overs per day very depressing, I must confess I do not enjoy the sight of four pace bowlers pounding away to basically the same fields. It is so monotonous unless, of course, wickets are tumbling and stumps flying. Because it limits the strokes the batsmen can play, it stifles the game and reduces the spectacle.

This truth was brought home to me in the sixties when Essex were playing Notts at Trent Bridge. I came in with Gordon Barker at tea, having batted for most of the morning and all afternoon against a depressing diet of four seamers with the 'keeper standing back and almost identical fields. Although Gordon and I had made quite a few runs – the pitch was tranquil and the over-rate at least eighteen per hour – neither of us had enjoyed batting. This had consisted very largely of the half-cock shot, the steer down

High, open and ugly describes Colin Croft's action.
Height and natural speed are allied to an unusual line caused by the angle
achieved by the wide placing of his left foot.

A perfect illustration of the difficulty batsmen have in facing Croft
– and also of why it *should* be nigh impossible for him to achieve
an lbw decision when a batsman plays a stroke.
To hit a leg stump with a well-pitched delivery, he would have to make
the ball pitch very wide of the off stump, although he has been known
to cut the occasional delivery back from leg.

through gully, the push off the legs, the occasional cut and the hook from Gordon when the bowlers fired the ball in short. It was the absence of variety which made batting so boring for us, but it must have been far worse for the few who had paid to watch.

F.S.T.   Something has to be done about these absurd over-rates. They're in danger of ruining Test cricket. West Indies were bad enough, but what went on during the England visit to India in 1981-82 was an absolute disgrace. Fining is largely a waste of time at international level, unless the fines exceed the large rewards. Something has to be done, but it should have been done at least five years ago. Unfortunately the ICC is not noted either for its administration or its speed in making decisions. However, it was good to see the ninety overs' per day minimum agreed by England and Australia in 1982-83, the only snag being that nobody appeared able to understand the small print.

T.E.B.   The ICC reminds me of the League of Nations, but even less effective. To my way of thinking, there are three alternative ways of attaining a realistic over-rate.
   (1)   The fielding side has to bowl a stipulated number of overs per day, and if this is not achieved the opposition are given an agreed number of runs.
   (2)   The fielding side has to send down a stipulated number of overs in a day. If this figure is not achieved, it has to continue bowling until it is. The danger here lies in that it could be used as a tactical weapon in certain circumstances.
   (3)   The number of overs the fielding side has to send down per session should be stipulated, and if the figure is not achieved, the fielding side must continue bowling throughout the intervals and after close of play. The umpires could deduct time lost through interruptions. This is a fairer method than (2) and should work, if only because people in England have a marked distaste for working overtime without extra pay.
   It is also worth mentioning that we already have a fixed twenty overs for the last hour of every match. Why not a fixed number for the first and the second?

F.S.T.   Going back to the West Indians, another reason for their success has been the number of genuinely fast bowlers they have waiting on the sidelines, all of them bursting to establish themselves and

178

start earning the big money that is now available in international cricket. This constant threat to the established bowlers means that no-one can afford to give less than his best or he runs the risk of losing his place. They all know they have to bowl well and take wickets, otherwise they'll be out and lose the rewards on offer.

.E.B. It is also true that life for pace bowlers is easier than it used to be. The ball today retains its shine and seam for much longer, with the result that bowlers are able to obtain movement both in the air and off the seam throughout the day. This has led to a noticeable increase in what might be termed medium-pace 'dobbers' and a corresponding decrease in spinners. In the past these 'phantom seamers' were meat and drink to any good batsman on a good pitch, but now they can trundle on economically, frequently making the ball deviate more than the slow bowler who spins it.

At The Oval immediately after the war, on a dry, fine day the seam bowler could expect no encouragement once the original gloss had worn from the ball. This usually had occurred by midway through the morning session, by which time the cover would be scuffed and the seam flattened or even almost non-existent. The genuine pace bowler still had his speed, but the medium-pacer had to rely on cut, change of pace and using the crease. These conditions applied even more overseas, where the rainfall was less and the sunshine more. An examination of a ball which was mounted for me in South Africa against any of those after 100 overs of international cricket today makes an intriguing comparison. Mine looks like a wizen old man; all the others will still have a pronounced seam and sufficient shine to encourage a swing bowler.

What is the reason for this considerable change in playing conditions? The main cause is undoubtedly the enormous improvement in cricket outfields. These days the majority are thickly carpeted with lush grass thanks to the application of artificial fertilisers. In the past they were much rougher with more bumps and bare patches. While the flat, grass carpets of today are a delight to field on, they do polish the ball when it is hit over them instead of roughing up the cover.

I may be wrong, but I also believe that the treatment to cricket balls by manufacturers has improved so that they retain their shine and seam longer, even if they do go out of shape rather more frequently than is desirable.

F.S.T.   In addition to far more favourable bowling conditions, I believe that the West Indian pacemen have been assisted by another important factor. Without wanting to detract from the ability of these fine bowlers, it has to be admitted that there is a shortage of world-class batsmen around at the present time. You can almost count the number of great international players on the fingers of one hand: Barry Richards, Greg Chappell and Glenn Turner, all near the end of their careers, Vivian Richards, Zaheer, Gavaskar, Miandad who has yet to reach his peak, Greenidge and, possibly, Gooch. The West Indian batting is not nearly as powerful as it usually has been since the war, and they are forced to depend over much on the genius of Richards, who is in an altogether different class from his colleagues.

There is not one Test team at the present time against which I would have minded bowling, and the Caribbean foursome have unquestionably been helped by coming up against so many players who were not of true Test calibre, let alone world class.

The Other Countries

Despite a stiff, rather awkward action, Peter Heine generated speed
and hostility, lift and movement off the seam by his height,
strength and patent dislike of batsmen.

Heine and Adcock

Peter Heine and Neil Adcock were the best, certainly the most menacing, pair of fast bowlers South Africa has produced since the Second World War; perhaps even in the whole of their history. Both stood well over six feet tall, and as they also had high actions they brought the ball down from a considerable height, enabling them to achieve considerable bounce even on a placid track.

Having opened against them throughout a South African tour, as well as facing them on numerous occasions in England, I had the opportunity to examine them at close quarters. As a duo I think they were probably the most physically menacing I encountered because both could make the ball lift unpleasantly from just short of a length. If I was fortunate enough to stay, I found myself playing most of their deliveries up around my waist. Their bouncers, too, tended to be more unpleasant than those of many bowlers of greater pace because they were able to make them rear to head high from closer to the unfortunate batsman.

Peter Heine was generally the more hostile of the two. He made his dislike of batsmen very obvious, and tended to become visibly angry if they had the temerity to stick around. This is well illustrated by what happened in a club match I saw in South Africa. Peter was playing for a club called the Pirates, well named I thought. An opposition batsman, having snicked a ball from Peter hard to the 'keeper, was given not out, and the sequel was entirely foreseeable. Two successive and vicious bouncers narrowly missed decapitating the wretched batsman, who was no more than a good club cricketer. I asked my South African companion why the batsman had not walked, to which he replied: 'Nobody ever walks against the Pirates.' They certainly play their club cricket hard in South Africa!

Peter was too stiff in his movements and too big to be an easy mover, so he lacked the grace of a Holding or the flow of a Trueman in his run-up. However, there was plenty of power and menace in his body action, and because he really thumped each delivery into the pitch, he often obtained movement off the seam as well as jarring the right hand of the batsman against the handle. Not infrequently, too, he scored a direct hit on the gloves.

Neil Adcock was a more complete bowler. He had a very straight gallop to the stumps and this took him, without a real jump, drag or deliberate rock-back, into and through his open-chested action. It was an unusual method, which I gather from some people who had seen Kortright, the great Essex fast bowler at the turn of the century, bowl was not dissimilar to his. Because of his style, Neil was more dependent on his run-up than most. And it meant that he had to come down on a left foot that was pointing straight at the batsman, rather than to fine-leg. Yet he was still able to swing the ball away from the right-hander, and he also bowled a very effective break-back. His away-swinger and 'nip-backer', in combination with the steepness of his delivery, the subsequent lift off the pitch, and his very considerable pace through the air, made him a match-winning fast bowler in his own right, as he demonstrated after his partner, Peter, had retired from the international scene. – T.E.B.

Heine and Adcock were not only among the most hostile opening pair to have played Test cricket, but they were also among the tallest. The combination of height and real pace enabled them to achieve an unusual amount of lift from even a docile pitch, while on a quick one they had the unpleasant habit of frequently hitting opposing batsmen – for whom they had little time – in the ribs.

I first encountered this pair when they came to England in 1955 as members of Jack Cheetham's splendid South African side which proved far stronger than had been expected. England eventually won the series by three Tests to two on a typical Oval 'turner' on which Laker and Lock picked up 15 wickets between them, Peter May having gone into the match with only two seamers, Statham and Bailey, because it was obviously going to be a spinner's wicket from the outset.

Although it took some time for the tourists to realise the fact, Peter Heine was especially effective under English conditions because he was able to make the ball deviate off the seam far more than he had been able to at home. He did not play in the First Test, which England won by an innings, but he was chosen for the Second, at Lord's. England elected to bat on a green wicket which Peter found very much to his taste, taking five wickets for 60 and having both May and Compton caught off balls which reared.

I had come into the England team at Lord's for Tyson, who was injured after taking eight wickets (including a spell of five for 5) in

Neil Adcock employed little rock-back in his high action.
As a result his left foot tended to point down the pitch,
but he was still able to swing the ball away in the air

the previous Test, but I was not picked again for a Test that summer, and as I missed the Yorkshire match against the tourists, I encountered Heine only once more in first-class cricket. That was playing for T. N. Pearce's XI, which Trevor captained, against the touring side at Scarborough. Consequently I did not really see enough of Peter to form a real judgement. He certainly looked a fine bowler with what seemed to me a mean and moody temperament. He did not mix easily.

Neil Adcock, who came back with the next South African side, was a very different character, apart from having the same dislike for opposing batsmen. An extrovert, he enjoyed life and people. What fascinated me about Neil's bowling was how he bowled an away-swinger, and a very good one, despite having an open-chested in-swinger's action. He was, in fact, the complete opposite of Alec Bedser, who bowled big in-swingers with a perfect out-swinger action. Neither made sense, but both certainly illustrated the danger of being too dogmatic about anything in cricket. – F.S.T.

Pollock and Procter

Mike Procter and Peter Pollock are usually remembered individually rather than as a partnership: the former as the finest all-rounder South Africa has produced and the latter as a high-quality international fast bowler. One is inclined to forget that for a brief period, covering part of one Test series and all of another, they formed the most devastating new-ball partnership in Test cricket for what, by 1970, had become the strongest team in the world, South Africa. The contrast between the pair naturally added to its effectiveness.

Peter Pollock was a fine fast bowler in his own right. He had a good, straight approach, a copybook action complete with toe-drag, excellent control and an aggressive temperament somewhat far removed from that of his batsman brother, the casually relaxed Graeme. His natural swing was away from the right-hander, and he also cut the ball back sharply from time to time, bowled very straight and had a distinctly nasty bouncer. Until the arrival of Procter in January 1967, he had been handicapped by South Africa's not having another pace bowler of the same calibre, and when they first teamed up, in the Third Test against Bobby Simpson's Australian side in Durban, Peter was already an experienced campaigner with a shrewd cricket brain and a particularly fine record for making that vital breakthrough with the new ball.

He was, in fact, the ideal partner for the young Procter who, at the time, was very fast and somewhat erratic, a case of brawn and brain in double harness. Mike, with his unusual 'hopper's' action, was inevitably an in-swinger, so there was never any problem between the pair over cross-winds. He was an immediate success, picking up seven wickets in his first Test and six in his second. With two more in the last Test of the series, he thus played a considerable part in South Africa's winning the rubber.

Because of the political issues that were to end with South Africa's exclusion from Test cricket, it was another three years before Pollock and Procter were able to share the new ball for their country again. Peter, almost thirty, was nearing the end of his career, but Mike by this time had established himself not only as a

Peter Pollock in the middle of his drag which, despite a long delivery stride,
enabled him to be very sideways on. His head is steady,
his eyes remain fixed on his target, and his balance is excellent.

fast bowler of the highest class but also as one who was very special. The renewal of their partnership proved catastrophic for what was reckoned to be a powerful Australian team. Bill Lawry's side had, after all, beaten West Indies in Australia in 1968-69 and India in India – a very different thing from beating them outside the sub-continent – *en route* to South Africa. They had also drawn with England in the last series the two countries had played in 1968.

It is difficult to think of any Australian team which has been more humiliated in a series, although to be fair the Australian administrators must be held partially responsible for the stupidity in arranging to go to South Africa, a very tough assignment, immediately after a hard tour to India. Australia were not just beaten by South Africa, they were massacred, losing all four Tests by the following margins: 170 runs, an innings and 129 runs, 307 runs and 323 runs. Procter took 26 wickets at a cost of 13.57 apiece, remarkable figures in a series in which the pitches were good and Australia's batting line-up consisted of Lawry, Stackpole, Ian Chappell, Walters, Redpath and Sheahan. Peter Pollock finished with a highly satisfactory 15 wickets a 17.20. Such impressive returns would suggest that the Pollock-Procter new-ball partnership was the best South Africa had ever fielded, and it is sad that politics prevented them from further opportunities against other countries.

I first faced Peter Pollock when the 1965 South Africans played Essex at Colchester. We were 59 for three when I arrived at the crease, Peter having removed both Michael Bear and Keith Fletcher for nought, and we limped to 87 for five. Happily, life became easier once Peter was rested and we reached a respectable 296 without undue difficulty. However, the fact that he was able to claim five wickets for 67 on a fast, true pitch does underline the problems he caused. He was quick enough to make me realise that from time to time it was safer to play him off the back foot. Furthermore he had plenty of stamina and could keep going for surprisingly long spells without any perceptible decrease in speed or accuracy.

Later, after retiring from the first-class scene, I was to come into contact with Peter on several occasions in Rothmans Cavaliers matches and similiar fixtures. I found him shrewd and intelligent, possessing a noticeably broader outlook than many of his countrymen. In this connection it is interesting that I never managed to be on the same cricket wavelength as his captain in 1965, Peter van

A delivery action which involved a hop from right foot to right foot
made it look as if Mike Procter bowled off the wrong foot.
Although he has still to release the ball, his left shoulder has already
fallen away and the left arm is of little importance.

Just how much Procter relied on a strong back, powerful right arm and a left knee which took enormous strain is apparent from this picture.

der Merwe; this despite never having had any difficulty with skippers from every other Test-playing country.

For a period after Gary Sobers had injured his knee, Mike Procter was clearly the most accomplished all-rounder in the world, and it must have been immensely frustrating to have had all that talent and yet been unable to employ it at the highest level of the game. In 1968 Mike decided to join Gloucestershire and for more than a decade he gave his adopted county outstanding service both as a player and as a captain. He was essentially one of those skippers who led from the front by personal example, rather than a subtle strategist, but then he had the ability to win matches virtually single-handed with bat, ball or both. He did so much for the club that it was often known as Proctershire, and there could be no greater compliment. Unlike his South African contemporary, Barry Richards, who became bored and disillusioned with the county circuit, perhaps because he loved batting more than the game itself, Mike Procter enjoyed his years with Gloucestershire and it showed. – T.E.B.

When South Africa paid their last visit to England, in 1965, and won the three-Test series one-nil, I was not chosen to play for England against them. It was said that van der Merwe, their captain, had instructed his players not to discuss either Brian Statham or myself because he did not want either of us to be in the Tests. In retrospect it is interesting to note that Brian was recalled for the last Test and took five wickets. As a result I saw Peter Pollock bowl on only one occasion and that was when the South Africans played Yorkshire at Sheffield. Still, I reckoned he was the quickest South African bowler I had encountered. What did really impress me was that he made the batsmen play the ball, realising unlike some fast bowlers the dual importance of attacking the stumps and of not wasting energy. What did puzzle me about him later on was that in spite of a fine sideways-on action, being over six feet tall and having a good physique, he seemed to be rather injury prone. That I could never understand.

I played against Mike Procter twice in 1968, which was my last season with Yorkshire and when we last won the County Championship. I had heard all about his all-round ability, but I was amazed when I first saw his unusual bowling action with the left arm playing no significant role. He had to rely on his right arm, his back and that unusual hop for his pace. His charge up to the wicket was very long, but like Bob Willis he was one of those bowlers who need their run-up to get the necessary impetus. Because he was so strong and fit, it did not take as much out of him as it would have most other people. However, his knee did take a great deal of strain, and it was not really surprising when it eventually let him down. The big surprise was that he was able to come back and bowl successfully again.

There have been a certain number of cricketers who bowled in-swingers which were sufficiently big for them, on occasions, to go round the wicket with the knowledge that they could justify an lbw appeal from a good-length delivery. Geoff Boycott was one of them, but Mike Procter is the only fast bowler I have seen with a sufficiently large in-swinger to make it worth his while going round the wicket for the same reasons as an off-spinner would on a turner.

For a long time Mike was, apart from Gary Sobers, the best all-rounder in the world, but unlike Gary he had no world stage. Apart from a few years in World Series Cricket in Australia, his exceptional talents were confined to domestic cricket in England and South Africa. This was sad because he had so much to give to the game. – F.S.T.

Richard Hadlee

Although cricket was firmly established in New Zealand long before the turn of the century, it has the least impressive playing record of all the Test-match countries, other than Sri Lanka which has only recently appeared on the international cricket scene. New Zealand had to wait until February 1978 to achieve their first Test victory over England, which, as their first Test-playing tour to England was in 1931, might be said to have been long overdue.

There are various reasons for this past lack of success in international cricket and for the small number of New Zealand players who warrant the label of great. Firstly, New Zealand is small with a population of about three million, though one could argue against this reason by presenting the example of Barbados, a minute island which has produced many more outstanding cricketers. However, cricket in Barbados is a national pastime, whereas in New Zealand Rugby Union, which unlike cricket has proved popular with the Maoris, has established itself as almost a second religion.

The climate, too, has played an important role. It is not dissimilar to England's and so there has always been a shortage of firm, fast, true pitches and an abundance of slow 'green tops'. Such conditions have tended to breed rather too many sound, grafting batsmen and honest medium and fast-medium seamers. Nor is New Zealand essentially a wealthy country, so the game has always suffered to some degree from lack of resources.

Finally, and probably the most important reason of all, was the isolation, which was far worse before the advent of regular air travel. One cannot help feeling that New Zealand's nearest neighbour, Australia, should have been more helpful in that period. Sir Donald Bradman, for instance, never batted there, and up until 1973-74 the two countries had played only one Test match, in 1945-46. Therefore, until recently, New Zealand cricketers have suffered from insufficient experience against class opposition.

One of the main strengths of New Zealand cricket has been their seamers, who have tended to be tall, gangling men with high arm actions, relying more on movement off the pitch than in the air.

The first really good New Zealand pace bowler I encountered

was Jack 'Bull' Cowie when he came to England in 1949 with Walter Hadlee's team. He was, at that time, no more than fast-medium, which was hardly surprising as he was then thirty-seven, but he had one of those body actions which exuded power and in his prime he obviously had been decidedly lively, as distinct from being a really fast bowler. Unfortunately I never had the opportunity of seeing him before the war, but I can well understand why so many of his contemporaries rate him as the finest quickie New Zealand has ever had, with a heart to match the strength of his big frame.

When I think of the New Zealand opening bowlers who followed Cowie, the most impressive, until the arrival of Richard Hadlee, were Tony MacGibbon, Dick Motz, Bruce Taylor, Richard Collinge and Dayle Hadlee. Tony, an angular six feet five, was able to make the ball lift awkwardly, gave nothing away and could keep going for long spells. However, he lacked real pace, and was in fact a replica of a good, reliable English seamer. Dick Motz was quicker, without being genuinely fast, but he was forced to retire through back injury while still in his prime. Dayle Hadlee was another whose career was cut short because of back trouble. Originally a highly promising fast-medium opening bowler, he was forced to cut down his pace and concentrate on swing, which he did to good effect until his injury became too painful. Richard Collinge had the height, a long run and sufficient pace to have become an outstanding, rather than good, Test-opening left-arm bowler had he only learnt how to bring the ball back into the right-hander.

Bruce Taylor was a tall, rather ungainly but effective fast-medium bowler who I always felt never quite fulfilled his potential. He was originally selected, with practically no first-class experience, for one of the most ambitious and demanding of all cricket tours. It contained four Tests in India, three in Pakistan and three in England. His international début at Calcutta in March 1965 could scarcely have been more dramatic: having lambasted the Indian attack for a memorable maiden century, he followed up with five wickets in India's first innings. But his most outstanding bowling performance came on New Zealand's tour to the West Indies in 1971-72. In four Tests, all of which were high-scoring draws on good pitches, Bruce captured a most impressive 27 wickets at only 17 apiece; but he was never able to approach that standard again.

These five Kiwi quickies were all good international pace bowlers, but none would I classify as great. Which brings me to Richard Hadlee, whom I believe to be the finest and the fastest of the New Zealand bowlers I have seen. There is no doubt that he is among the most respected and feared quick bowlers in the world, with over 170 Test wickets to his credit as New Zealand's leading wicket-taker. His other records for New Zealand at international level include the highest number of wickets in a Test match and in a Test innings. However, such statistical feats must be considered in respect of the era in which he has played, a time when there have been so many more Test matches. Jack Cowie may not have been as good a fast bowler as Richard, but he unquestionably was a very fine one. Yet he played only nine Test matches, in which he took a very creditable 45 wickets at just over 21 apiece, whereas Richard, when he returned to England with the 1983 Kiwis, had already made 46 appearances.

Richard joined Nottinghamshire in 1978, initially as a replacement for Clive Rice, whom the County Committee had prematurely sacked for signing for World Series Cricket. Before Rice was able to obtain redress in the High Court, the club wisely changed its decision, which meant that, until Richard joined that season's New Zealand touring party, Notts had a lethal opening attack, as well as two fast-scoring batsmen. This South African-New Zealand combination, aided and abetted by some lively pitches at Trent Bridge, was the chief reason why Nottinghamshire won the 1981 County Championship, in the course of which Richard took 105 wickets at a cost of only 14.89, making him easily the most devastating bowler in county cricket that summer. As he also hit 745 runs, often spectacularly, his adopted county could justifiably claim that they had had quite exceptional value for money.

The success Richard has enjoyed in county cricket further underlines his quality. The difference a fast bowler – or preferably a pair – makes to any team is enormous. Not only is he a match-winner, but he will often demoralise the opposition with his speed and hostility. It is noticeable how some highly accomplished batsmen lose their confidence once the ball starts flying around their ears and they are in danger of receiving an occasional painful blow. What is more, the bowler will instinctively smell them out. Had I been looking for a young county batsman likely to make runs against West Indies or Australia in the early 1980s, I would first have studied his record against Nottinghamshire. – T.E.B.

Down and across goes Richard Hadlee's bowling arm in the first
stride of a copybook follow-through. The head, however, remains
steady and his eyes follow the ball.

Richard Hadlee is a product of one of the great cricketing families. His father Walter was not only a fine batsman in the classical mould, but he was also one of New Zealand's outstanding captains and a leading administrator. All Richard's four brothers played cricket, and one of them, Dayle, would have taken part in more than 26 Tests if injury hadn't interrupted his career.

In my opinion Richard is the best fast bowler New Zealand, has had and, though he has looked decidedly unhappy batting against pace bowling, he must come into the all-rounder class. He was the first of his countrymen to complete the double in Test cricket, and in 1979-80 he scored a somewhat improbable century off 92 deliveries from a West Indian attack which in effect relied entirely on that fearsome pace quartet of Roberts, Holding, Garner and Croft.

When I first saw Richard bowl, I liked his body action, which was sideways-on and easy. The first virtue enabled him to move the ball away from the bat; the second meant that he did not have to strain for extra pace, and also made him quicker than he looked. I felt, however, that his run-up was too long, and since he shortened it after joining Notts I believe he has become an even better bowler. He has certainly become much more accurate. Although there was plenty of speed and hostility in his early days of international cricket, he was often, like most young pacemen, wild and erratic. Today he seldom, if ever, wastes his time and energy bowling wide of the stumps. He makes the batsman play, and as he moves the ball sometimes in the air and sometimes off the pitch, he is consequently picking up even more wickets. For a time in the early 1980s, he could be considered, in all conditions and on all types of pitches, the finest fast bowler in the world; though I would hasten to add that my first choice would have been Joel Garner, who admittedly was fast-medium rather than fast.

Richard, tall and wiry rather than big, displays a quick temper when bowling, which means that he, quite rightly, does not like opposing batsmen, at least while they are at the crease. On the other hand he definitely does like bowling, and is prepared to perform even on those occasions when he is not fully fit – unlike some members of the fast-bowling brigade I have known. This professional attitude is of great value to his adopted county and to New Zealand, who rely so much not only on his bowling but also on his presence in the side. The danger, though, is that he will continue playing instead of taking a rest to recover, and this could seriously delay his return to complete fitness. – F.S.T.

Imran Khan and Kapil Dev

The quality of much of the international cricket played by England, India and Pakistan in the summer of 1982 was not very high. England, without those players who had taken part in the South African adventure the previous winter, were unable to find a recognised pair of opening batsmen, lacked a high-class spinner and were able to field only two bowlers – Willis and Botham – who had shown themselves capable of winning a Test. Nevertheless, under their new captain, Bob Willis, they managed to beat India very easily and took a close, interesting series against Pakistan by two Tests to one. Cricket lovers were fortunate in one, or rather three, respects in that they did have the chance to see and compare the three most successful international all-rounders their respective countries have produced.

I have never before seen three all-rounders of such high quality playing Test cricket in the same summer. What makes it even more remarkable was that all three were not only the main strike bowlers of their respective teams but were also good enough to be chosen purely for their batting ability.

T.E.B. It is certainly rare to find players at this level who are quite so outstanding in all three departments of the game. Of the two visitors, who impressed you most?

F.S.T. It's hard to say, because both are great cricketers in their own right. Imran was the sounder, but I found Kapil Dev more exciting. With the bat, he was prepared, indeed eager, to take on Botham and Willis when India were struggling, and more often than not he came out on top. Imran, on the other hand, tended to steer his team to safety with watchful defence and the occasional brilliant stroke. Kapil also had the disadvantage of playing for much the weaker team. At the moment he is technically not nearly such a good batsman as Imran, but he is certainly a more spectacular and stronger striker of the ball.

T.E.B. The biggest weakness of Indian cricket over the years has been

Imran Khan's big leap at the end of a long, probably over-long run-up is a feature of his bowling and plays an important part in the pace and lift he achieves. It also enables him to maximise his left arm throughout his action.

their inability to produce fast bowlers. Of course the Indian climate and pitches do not encourage fast bowling, while both the physique and the diet of so many Indians are unsuitable. Their lack of adequate pace bowling has proved an especially big disadvantage away from home, and it has also meant that Indian batsmen tend to be uncomfortable against real speed, especially abroad, because they do not face enough of it.

Rather strangely, two of the best Indian pace bowlers came on their very first tour to England, in 1932: Mahomed Nissar and Amar Singh. Nissar was probably, certainly for the first few overs, the fastest of all Indian bowlers, while Amar Singh, who was fast-medium with a short run and moved the ball, was arguably the best. Since then there has been Desai, who was small and slight, quite sharp, and had a somewhat suspect action. Others like Divecha and Phadkar would certainly not worry batsmen with their pace, but now Kapil Dev has arrived to end the famine. What do you make of him as a fast bowler?

S.T. To my mind, Kapil is a good, very good, quick bowler, but not a really fast one. However, he has not made that big mistake of trying to be one. He's just quick enough to get bastmen thinking about playing him off the back foot. Bigger and much stronger than the majority of Indian seamers, he has a pleasing high action and a sensible run-up which allows him to bowl for very long spells. This, of course, he has to do, because his team is short of penetrative bowling support.

Kapil's height enables him to rap opposing batsmen on the gloves from time to time, and he bowls a natural late out-swinger, makes the odd ball come back sharply off the seam, and possesses a lively, as distinct from lethal, bouncer. He is the best opening bowler from India I have seen, and he has not yet reached his peak. His biggest danger is being bowled into the ground. This happened several times in 1982 when lack of alternatives forced Sunil Gavaskar to employ his only shock bowler also as his tireless, uncomplaining stock bowler.

E.B. Since they acquired Test status, it is noticeable that Pakistan have been much more successful than India in coping with fast bowling for the obvious reason that they themselves have produced a number of accomplished seamers.

In the early days their outstanding seamer and arguably their

A nicely balanced jump at the end of a sensible run-up brings
Kapil Dev into a sideways-on position with his back beginning to arch.
Although his head is looking over his left shoulder,
it has swung too far back for his action to be classical.

finest was Fazal Mahmood, who was, I suppose, Pakistan's Alec Bedser. Although not as quick, Fazal, like Alec, bowled in-swingers, a very good leg-cutter, and maintained an immaculate line and length. His pace was closer to medium than fast. I faced Fazal for the first time in 1954, when Pakistan made their first visit to England, playing against them in the first three Tests. We won the Second at Trent Bridge by an innings and plenty, and the other two were drawn because rain prevented play on three days each time. In the First and Third Tests, Pakistan failed to reach three figures in their first innings, and so for the final Test, at The Oval, our Selectors, regarding it as a formality and with a view to trying out players for Australia, left out our leading bowler, Alec Bedser, and myself. They also included Jim McConnon ahead of Jim Laker, which made far less sense. The outcome was that Pakistan won the match by 24 runs and tied the series, thanks to the bowling of Fazal who took six for 53 and six for 46 in conditions that were tailor-made for Alec.

S.T.   I played against Fazal in the Fourth Test of 1962, when he was flown out as a replacement after two of Pakistan's opening bowlers had broken down. By then he was no more than medium pace and ambled up a few paces, but he still took three of the five wickets which fell and sent down 60 overs for 130 runs, which was not a bad performance considering our lads put together 428. Peter Parfitt's century was his sixth in seven innings against them.

T.B.   Fazal was, of course, at his most formidable on the mat in Pakistan, where his ability to cut the ball off the seam either way made him one of the most effective bowlers in the world. His figures at Karachi in 1956-57, when Pakistan won their first Test against a strong Australian side, certainly support this assessment: 27–11–34–6 in the first innings and 48–17–80–7 in the second. He was also the key bowler when Pakistan beat West Indies in a three-Test series in Pakistan in 1958-59 and had captured 20 wickets when Pakistan lost in the Caribbean the previous season.

S.T.   Among other effective new-ball bowlers from Pakistan there was Asif Masood, who in the right conditions really could make the ball swing. I must confess, though, that I remember him best for that chassé at the start of his run-up. It was straight out of 'Come Dancing'! Mahmood Hussain was a useful fast-medium in-swinger, and I have always had a high regard for the unpredictable Sarfraz Nawaz, who overcame the weakness of a stiff, rather awkward approach and body action by sheer physical strength and determination. He may look ungainly, but he bowls quickly and achieves a considerable amount of movement off the seam and plenty of bounce. When he's in the mood, he can be distinctly hostile.

However, the most feared, and the fastest, of all the Pakistan bowlers to date is without doubt Imran Khan. He is genuinely quick – one of the fastest in the world – and is able to beat batsmen by sheer speed through the air. His action is slightly open and his natural swing is into the right-hander, but he has also learnt to bowl the ball that holds its own or even leaves the bat, which makes him that much more formidable. His problem is that he is easily the most deadly bowler in the Pakistan side, and so inevitably he has to bowl too often, and in too long spells, if his team are to win.

T.E.B.   I have no doubt that Pakistan would have won the series against England in 1982 if Sarfraz, even though he is nearing the end of his career, had been fit throughout. What a difference he would have made in that very close final Test when Imran took the new ball in the first innings with an emergency replacement, Ehtesham-ud-Din, who would have been more at home in club cricket than a Test match. I think Imran's failure, as captain, to realise the potential of Mudassar as a medium-pace seamer, especially after the havoc he caused at Lord's, was another fatal mistake.

F.S.T.   Obviously a fully fit Sarfraz would have made all the difference, but I still think Imran might have won the First Test at Edgbaston had he bowled a full length and tried to swing the ball against the England tail, which staged a splendid rally. He appeared to be more interested in trying to hit the two Bobs, Willis and Taylor, than getting them out, and that was equally fatal to Pakistan's chances. In my opinion Imran's run-up is too long, and it is interesting that when from time to time he uses a shortened version there is no noticeable reduction of pace.

T.E.B.   Although there were times when Imran, as a very overworked player and an inexperienced captain, made mistakes – I believe that if Mike Brearley had led Pakistan, they would have won the series – there can be no denying that few players have ever given more to their country than Imran with bat, ball and in the field.

Index

Acknowledgements

Picture credits
BBC Hulton Picture Library: 40, 57, 113, 121, 185.
Central Press Photos: 44, 48, 112, 150.
Patrick Eagar: 21, 32, 82, 89, 94, 97, 101, 104, 105, 128, 134, 135, 139, 143, 163, 168, 174, 176, 177, 181, 188, 190, 191, 200, 202.
Ken Kelly: 79, 171.
MCC: 29.
Sport and General Press Agency: 62, 70, 125, 182.
Topham: 28, 117, 155.

The photographs introducing each section are as follows:
p. 21 Mike Hendrick of England, Derbyshire and Nottinghamshire.
p. 101 Rodney Hogg of Australia and South Australia.
p. 143 Malcolm Marshall of West Indies, Barbados and Hampshire.
p. 181 Bruce Taylor of New Zealand, Canterbury and Wellington.